BRAS
AND
PENUS
ON A
DATE

BRAS
AND
PENUS
ON A
DATE

A Guide for Surviving the 7 Stages
of Dating to Create a Loving,
Lasting, Subpoena-Free Relationship

DEBBIE KASPER, Su.C.*
ELLIOT SULLIVAN, Su.C.*

Illustrations by Raymond Larrett

Ship of Fools

An Imprint of Sullivan & Foster Publishing, New York
An Entagon Communications Company

* **Stand-up Comic**

Ship of Fools Books
An imprint of Sullivan & Foster Publishing
An Entagon Communications Company
173 West 81st Street, Lower Level
New York, NY 10024

Cover design: Topanga Graphics, Inc.
Book design: Alan Barnett, Inc.

ISBN 1-890410-14-4

Books may be ordered in quantity from your local bookseller or
you may order single or bulk quantities by phoning AES Books:
Toll Free: 1-800-717-2669
All credit cards accepted.
E-mail: info@aesbooks.com

To Anna Collins, the Brassierian Queen

— *Elliot Sullivan*

To Cindy Bee Kramer, for being
everything I'd like to one day

— *Debbie Kasper*

Contents

Acknowledgments

To **Pat Sierchio** for his love, compassion, and mostly, his jokes; to **Paul Lyons** for his outstanding input; to **Olivia Mellan-Shapiro, Dena Seigel, Kenneth Saltman,** and **Robin Goodman** for their insightful comments and suggestions; to **Gary Larson** and **Jeanie Curtiss** for guarding the fort against "wolves, termites, and floods" while the book was being written; to **Alan Barnett** for working when he should have been sleeping; to **Judy Pokras** for minding our Ps and Qs instead of her Zs; to **John Gray** for his humanity and wonderful sense of humor. And, above all, special thanks to **Anna Collins,** without whom this book would not be possible.

Women are from Bras, Men are from Penus

NOT THAT LONG AGO, in a galaxy not that far away, lived two opposite civilizations. One lived on the planet Bras and the other on the planet Penus. Little did they know they were headed on a collision course for each other. Everyone was doomed to destruction except the planets' lawyers, who financed their escape through personal injury law suits.

As the planets got closer and closer, one of the inhabitants on Penus, a Penusian, was looking through his Penuscope,™ which is like a telescope, only when extended, a lot smaller. He saw the planet Bras and, much to his delight, spied a bevy of beautiful bare-bottomed, bosomy Brassierians bathing in brightly bejeweled bronze bathtubs.

He immediately — after watching for two and a half hours — called his buddies to see this incredible sight. The Penusians started clamoring to get a look at the Brassierians. After taking many turns watching, the Penusians unanimously decided to take more turns watching. So they continued to watch until their eyes crossed and their wrists got really really tired.

The Penusians had to meet these gorgeous Brassierians at any cost, unless it meant missing the playoffs on TV. So, being the fix-it-build-it widget types, they constructed the *Starship Enterthighs* in the hopes they would boldly go where no Penusian had gone before — namely, the laundromat.

The Enterthighs was equipped with a 30,000 Mhz Pentium computer, a forty-on-the-floor plutonium-injected engine, and a pair of foam dice hanging from the rear-view mirror. It also had a 520-inch remote-controlled TV capable of receiving 84,329 channels — though there *still* wasn't anything worth watching.

The trip to Bras would have normally taken three light years, but it took seven because the Penusians were too *egotesticle* to ask for directions. Eventually, however, they landed on Bras and everybody had to pee really bad.

The Penusians and Brassierians took to each other right from the start. They were enthralled with each other's differences. Each had something that bulged and swelled in a different way. For the Brassierians it was their breasts. For the Penusians it was their egos.

For a while, everything went along great because they were madly in love. Love being blind, they found their way around each other using Braille. This gave rise to sex and things started going along even better. They had great sex, great food, great sex — a little burping and farting here and there — great sex. They couldn't ask for more.

Then they all decided to travel to the planet Earth. Once on Earth, however, they developed *selective nausea*. They wouldn't be nauseous all the time — only when they were with each other. Pretty soon the touching turned into poking. The poking turned into punching. The punching turned into pounding. And the pounding turned into short-range nuclear weapons.

To survive they devised strategies, tactics, schemes, maneuvers, tricks, ploys, games, ruses, gimmicks, deceits, subterfuges, skullduggery and espionage. There were even times when they were subtle and indirect.

••

**Men will never understand women and women
will never understand men — and that is the one thing
that men and women will never understand.**

••

Penusians wrote songs about their predicament, such as, "A Pretty Girl is Like a Malady." Brassierians wrote articles in women's magazines such as, "When I Was Dating, He Was My Ideal. Now that We're Married, He's My Ordeal."

Each tried desperately to understand the other. Penusians tried to understand why Brassierians were interested in the alphahydroxy content of their new moisturizer and the best place to get a sugarless double-mocha half-caf cappuccino with fat-free nondairy topping. Brassierians tried to understand why Penusians would be interested in the new defensive lineman for the Bills and who got the most R.B.I.'s in the World Series in 1958.

They tried reading self-help books like: *You Just Don't Understand, How to Enhance Your Interpersonal Communication, What You Thought You Heard Was not, in Fact, What I Actually Meant,* and finally, *Hey Asshole, What the Fuck Are You Trying to Say?*

What both sides never realized is that men will never understand women, and women will never understand men — and that is the one thing that men and women will never understand.

Introduction

Are you lonely, miserable, and heartbroken? Then you're one of two things: you're either married or you're single.

If you're lonely and miserable, isn't it high time you found someone you can be lonely and miserable with? That's why you sprang $9.95 for this book — to find the perfect person to be miserable with. Or at least someone you can *make* lonely and miserable. Or someone already miserable that you can help make lonely, too.

After reading this book, just don't expect to be running around mating, dating, and procreating. You're setting your goals too high. Lower your standards and, with any luck, you'll end up lying, spying, and testifying. That much we can promise you.

Just don't ask us about love or happiness or romance, because we've never experienced them — though we did see some good movies about the subject: *Bride of Frankenstein, The St. Valentine's Day Massacre,* and *Psycho.*

They say, "It's better to have loved and lost than to never have loved at all." We say, "It's better to have loved and lost than to be run over by a tractor-trailer — but not by much."

So get out there and start hurting people! And if you get hurt, hurt back! We mean now. That's right; put the book down and start. You already know as much as we do, unless you've seen someone naked in the past year, in which case you might know more. So what are you waiting for?

All right, then continue reading, but remember, we don't have any answers. We are not scientists, psychologists, philosophers, or people even more qualified to help others — bartenders! We're no better than you are. Well, maybe a little better, but not much. If you really need help, buy John Gray's book — he's a professional.

And just between you and us, we're also lonely and miserable. We don't get along with anybody — especially with each other. We couldn't even sit in the same room to write this book. We couldn't even sit on the same coast. We're so mismatched, our computers aren't even speaking to each other. Debbie is a Brassierian and Elliot is a Penusian, and you know what that means: the only thing we have in common is that we're both carbon-based life forms. And until we get the results of our recent physicals, we're not even sure about that.

So brace yourself. Fasten your seat belt. And strap on your bullet-proof vest. You are about to navigate the seven stages of dating. You are already in the first stage: DESPERATION. This is when your love life *rots*.

1

Desperation
When your love life rots

You're alone. You're miserable. You're desperate. And you're heartbroken — but not housebroken, because you leave your shit wherever you go. Yes, you're alone, but you sleep naked anyway just for practice. You've been alone so long the voices in your head have laryngitis from talking so much.

It's been so long since you've had sex that everything reminds you of it. You're beginning to think "Farmer in the Dell" is a dirty song, and every time you get to the part about "the wife taking the sheep," you get hot.

Misery loves company, but desperation happens alone.

The good news about your loneliness is that you're probably in good physical shape because you're still trying to nab someone. Most married people have let themselves go. (If you think this is a gross generalization, read on. The book is chock full of them.)

But do note that marriage leads to:

- Becoming fat

- Children

- More fat

- More children

- Mortgages

- More fat children

- Hemorrhoids

- Fred and Ethyl Mertz hairdo's

- Seeing your fat children every other weekend

- Tracking down dead beat dads for not feeding their fat children

Most married couples seem to treat each other badly. They take the relationship for granted. They don't know how lucky they are

Before   After

to have found someone who is devoted to making them miserable. Let's face it. Misery loves company, but desperation happens alone.

Signs You've Been Alone Too Long

Have you been single too long? There are ways of telling. One glaring one is that you are reading this book. **Other signs are:**

Women

- You see a "Jesus is Coming" billboard and you pull over to put on makeup.

- A homeless man cat-whistles you and you pull over to put on makeup.

- You get a breast exam — you don't need one, you're just lonely.

- You dream about your eighth-grade boyfriend, but in your dream he's *still* in the eighth grade and you still have a crush on him.

- You order Japanese food and slip into a kimono before the delivery boy arrives.

- You take yourself out to dinner before you have your way with yourself.

- Even in your fantasies Prince Charming stands you up.

- You phone the Jehovah's Witnesses to ask why they haven't been around lately.

Men

- You watch Judge Judy, hoping her robe might fly open.

- You won't masturbate; you're not ready to make the commitment.

Hmmm... I wonder if he's married...

- You think you can attract chicks with your new tee-shirt that says, IT'S NOT MY EGO THAT NEEDS STROKING!

- You call information and when the operator can't find the number, you tell her she's a cock teaser.

- You get a tooth filled just so the dental assistant will put her fingers in your mouth.

- A Jehovah's Witness comes to your door — and you marry her.

Daily Meditations For Lonely People

Repeat the following phrases until someone *you* love breaks up with someone *they* love.

Monday
"I'm lonelier than a Siamese twin at a singles dance."

Tuesday
Keep saying, "boo-hoo, boo-hoo" until someone comes along and helps you.

Wednesday
"Please God, send me a partner, and I promise I won't kill this one."

Thursday
"It's not my fault everyone is a complete asshole."

Friday
"I've lowered my standards, God. Now I'll settle for someone who can at least *stand* erect."

Saturday
"God, you make me sick. I don't believe in you anyway. If you exist, how do you explain the Beanie Baby craze?"

Sunday
"God, I'm sorry about what I said yesterday. I was upset. I'm not asking you for a mate. I'm just asking you for enough morphine until one comes along."

....

Strange bedfellows are better than no bedfellows at all.

....

The Clock Keeps Ticking

There is a statistic that women over the age of 40 have a greater chance of getting kidnapped by a terrorist than getting married — which is good, because most terrorists are single. Perhaps the woman would be better off with the terrorist. The average kidnapping lasts twice as long as the average relationship. She could count on him to be at her side day and night. And when it was all over, she could sell the story to *Lifetime* television for a million dollars. *Lifetime* loves kidnappings with happy endings. After all,

Hi honey, I'm home.

a kidnapping is a relationship too, and strange bedfellows are better than no bedfellows at all. Just don't *marry* the kidnapper because the story would lose its edge — unless immediately after, you kidnap and murder *him*.

The Grass Is Always Greener

Life is unfair. Make that your mantra and you won't spend your entire life *really* miserable, just moderately miserable. It seems like everyone is a lot happier than you. And often *they really are*. The last thing you want to do is go out and meet people. You feel out of sorts, distant, aloof, discombobulated. You feel there is something wrong with you, and all you can think about is becoming combobulated.

The trouble is, the more alienated you feel, the more you push others away. The more you push others away, the more they want to avoid you. The more they want to avoid you, the more alienated you feel. This goes on and on until even your therapist stops returning your calls. It's a no-brainer. People who feel alienated are just no fun to be around.

The thing to realize is that *everybody* feels alienated — everybody is as screwed up as you are. Yes, the grass is always greener — because your neighbor uses astro turf. So don't be so hard on yourself. Leave that for your next partner.

People Who Fear Intimacy

Fear of intimacy is a serious disease. Some people want to be left alone so badly they stop bathing, just so they can stink. Smelling badly is rarely an accident or an oversight. It takes work and dedication. If you meet someone who stinks, run away — they fear intimacy.

....

Men don't like sex in space because afterwards they can't get up and leave.

....

These people-repellers are easy to spot. They cover their bras with barbed wire. They have tattoos that say things like, GO AWAY and I WAS DUMPED BY SATAN. They live in antisocial places like huts in Montana and space stations. ***Warning:*** Just because a man is up in space, doesn't mean he wants to take the relationship to the next level. If you're a woman, try hard to avoid him, even if you have this kinky fantasy that one day you'll get drunk on vodka and tang (a Harvey Spacebanger) and have sex in weightlessness. It's not gonna happen. Besides, men don't like sex in space because afterwards they can't get up and leave.

And remember women, just because you're weightless, doesn't mean you look thinner.

Somewhere along the way some shrink told these people to practice intimacy on a plant, an animal, or even bacteria, and they promptly realized they like animals better. (They actually preferred the bacteria, but they kept breaking the petri dish during sex.)

How to Tell If You're with Someone Who Fears Intimacy

To find out if someone fears intimacy, it is important to read the signs. For instance, if a sign in their yard says, MY DOG MAY NOT BITE, BUT I DO, they probably fear intimacy.

Another sign is that they live alone with 17 cats and one day grab a rifle and find a tower. When reporters interview neighbors after the mass killings, the neighbors always say, "He never bothered anybody." *This is an even bigger sign.* Normal people bother others all the time. If you know someone who's not bothering you, call the police. And don't stand under a tower.

....

Normal people bother others all the time. If you know someone who's not bothering you, call the police.

....

If you play your cards right, this could be your lucky night, lady.

Why Animals Make Better Companions Than People

Some lonely people say pets make better companions. Some of the reasons they give are:

- Pets don't care which CD's they get in the break-up.

- You can blow off Valentine's Day and they'll still lick you.

- They *never* leave their dirty underwear around.

- The toilet seat is always exactly how you left it.

- Pets don't know when it's their birthday.

- They actually *like* being locked out of the house.

To Date or Mastur-Date?

Dating can be more tortuous than a POW camp. If North Vietnamese interrogators threatened U.S. Marines to go on dates, the Marines would have confessed to everything, including the framing of Roger Rabbit. McArthur said, "War is hell." We say McArthur was a big baby. War is nothing compared to dating.

With dating so depressing, it occurs to many they actually might have a better time if they just stayed home and *masturdated*. Men like to masturdate because afterwards they can say they were the best they ever had. Women rarely masturdate. Many have low self-esteem so they don't think they're worth the trouble.

While there are social and psychological considerations in deciding whether to date or masturdate, often the overriding considerations are financial:

AVERAGE DATING COSTS FOR MEN PER DATE

Meal costs	$85.62
Alcohol costs during the date	$18.31
Alcohol costs to recover from the date	$44.13

Tip to bartender for listening to you
complain about date. $10.00

Entertainment costs to cover up boring date. $61.29

Travel costs to quickly get away after date $24.00

Total Cost Per Date **$243.35**

MASTURDATING COSTS FOR MEN

Kleenex for cleanup . . . . $.08

DATING COSTS FOR WOMEN

Actual dating expenses
(men should pick up expenses) . . . . $.00

Phone bill to call every woman she knows
bragging she has a date. $300.00

Phone bill to call every woman back
bitching about how badly the date went. $300.00

Total **$600.00**

MASTURDATING COSTS FOR WOMEN

Actual masturdating costs . . . . $.00

Therapy costs for guilt. $600.00

Total **$600.00**

This analysis should help you decide how to spend your money
— and where to put your hands.

WHY THE BEST PERSON TO DATE IS YOURSELF

There are tremendous advantages of going out by yourself *alone*.
The reasons are:

For Guys

- You can now afford two movies for the price of one. And if the movie is dark enough, you can touch your own Milk Dud and no one will ever know.

- If you meet a "babe" while you're out, you can hit on her without arousing jealousy — until you meet a better babe while flirting with the first babe.

- If you arrive late, you won't have to put up with a marathon nag-a-thon, ruining the plot of *Die Hard IV*.

- You don't have to bother being nice. You'll have sex with yourself later anyway.

For Gals

- You don't have to sit through another stupid *Lethal Weapon* sequel, agreeing with your moronic date that, "Yeah that could really happen."

- You don't have to feign the appetite of a gnat. You can eat like a wild boar — spilling, grunting, and snorting.

- You don't have to work on your "sexcuses" why you won't be inviting him in after the date.

- In bed that night you can find your G-spot quickly without giving your date an electronic honing device.

Why Single People are Single

Many people insist they like being single. Unfortunately, for many of them this is just a façade. Their defense mechanisms are working harder than a one-winged fly on a mound of buffalo shit.

The longer you're single, the more you're convinced you like being single. This is a trap. People who have undergone a lot of dental work also say, "Root canals don't really hurt." It's all relative. Root canals don't hurt as much as, say, listening to a Yoko Ono love songs CD, but they are painful — and so is being single. It's the kind of pain that only an intravenous drip of Jack Daniels can address.

Most people don't like being single. Most people do like Jack Daniels.

Don't You Want Somebody to Love?

These words, sung by the Jefferson Airplane, express the human dilemma perfectly. Everybody is desperate to hook up with somebody. We burst into relationships like the Americans storming Normandy — and the casualty rate is just as high.

After a string of failures, even laboratory mice are smart enough to try a different route through the maze. Then again, mice are also smart enough to avoid dating. They claim they'd rather get caught in a glue trap and flushed down the toilet than go out on a date.

So what's the answer to the question, "Don't you want somebody to love?" It's usually:

- No thank you, I'm trying to cut back.

- I just don't have that kind of money right now.

- No, I want somebody to love *me,* the hell with them.

- No, I want somebody to *use.*

Yes, people think that love makes the world go 'round, but it's not true. Love make the world go berserk. It's Häagen Dazs that makes the world go 'round — or at least *grow* round.

The Vicious Cycle of Love

The only one who understood love was Plato (the Greek philosopher, not the children's modeling clay). He called it a "grave mental disease." Plato may have swapped smutty stories about Athena and hung around naked in the baths with Socrates, but he was pretty smart about love and marriage. In fact, he coined the phrase, "It's not the size of the boat, it's the motion of the ocean."

Sure, the early stages of love are euphoric, but anything feels good at first. Even Chinese water torture kind of tingles in the beginning. But it's that constant drip...drip...drip...drip that drives you stark raving mad. And it's the same thing with the stages of love.

We get stuck in a vicious cycle. We're attracted to a person who is bad for us. Or we'll idealize our partner by putting the face of someone like Brad Pitt or Cameron Diaz on their body so we can fall in love with a movie star. And the love lasts as long as a movie — two hours and eight minutes.

Golly, this has been the best two hours and eight minutes of my life, Jeeter.

Attracted to Mr. or Ms. Wrong

Unfortunately, when Mr. Wrong dates Ms. Wrong, two wrongs don't make a right. Let's face it. Women don't want nice guys. Most women are attracted to the kind of guy who looks like he might snap at any moment. Then he'll belt her one and blame her for it. For some mysterious reason, this is sexy.

**When Mr. Wrong dates Ms. Wrong,
two wrongs don't make a right.**

Although most women *claim* to be liberated, many of them just have big mouths. People confuse that with liberation. Deep down many women *want* a man to tell her what to do. Then she gets to say her favorite line, "Fuck off, you macho pig."

Man's self-image

Women Have Low Self-Esteem

A woman is attracted to Mr. Wrong for one reason: she has low self-esteem. She's often attracted to a man so self-centered that during oral sex he calls out his own name. And if he calls her the wrong name in bed, she gives him three more guesses.

Low self-esteem is the one thing that separates us from other mammals. You never see an elephant at the zoo saying, "Does my ass look fat?"

Self-Esteem Exercises for Women

Look in the mirror naked and say:

"You're beautiful, and I love you."

Woman's self-image

If you can't say this at the beginning, start out with:

"You look like you're smuggling potatoes under that skin, and you make me sick."

And eventually, as you grow, this will transform itself into the phrase:

"You're beautiful...and I love potatoes."

Men Are Immature

Men don't suffer from low self-esteem. Men are immature. Men are so immature, they will pay to log on to Internet sights that peek under women's skirts with a hidden video camera.

If men were mature, they would be doing the peeking themselves, instead of hiring a peek-a-boo hit man. Think about it. You never see women selling hidden pictures of guys scratching their jock straps in a locker room.

Because men are immature, they're attracted to the wrong women. A man wants a foxy chick to show he's got big *cojones*. The truth is he's got no cojones — *anymore!* The foxy chick snatched them and keeps them in her freezer next to her fish sticks while she reads *Women Who Run with the Wolves, and then Eat Them*.

Searching for Mr./Ms. Right

People are always looking for the perfect person. Quite frankly, the perfect person wouldn't want *you*. Very often people who seem perfect really are perfect — perfect assholes!

Others think that if you can't find Mr./Ms. Right, you should settle for Mr./Ms. Alright, or Mr./Ms. Right-for-Now. The trouble is even Mr./Ms. Not-that-Bad is not that good. You're setting your sights too high.

What a good little low-life you are!

This is why you should look for Mr./Ms. Better-than-Nothing. This way, right from the start, you're not plagued by high expectations. You expect them to be losers, low lifes, and burger flippers. Then, whenever they do something remotely intelligent, like fetch a stick, you're pleased. And you reward them with a pat on the head and a small piece of cheese.

••

Even Mr./Ms. Not-that-Bad is not that good....That is why you should look for Mr./Ms. Better-than-Nothing.

••

So the choices are clear. You can settle for nothing — and don't get us wrong; nothing is good. We have a very high regard for nothing. If you have nothing, think of all the heartaches and headaches you *avoid*. Every time you walk in the door you don't have to answer to the Spanish Inquisition. Nobody will care where you've been. And you'll save a lot of money on cheese.

But if you'd like to find someone who is better than nothing, you are ready for the next stage of dating: PROTECTION. So arm yourself with pepper spray, call up your lawyer, and slip into something uncomfortable — like a condom, because in this stage the last thing you need to worry about is a bunch of tiny *tots*.

2

Protection

When you don't want tots

So you're ready to get ready to start thinking about, maybe, planning on beginning to — not right now, but soon — maybe date again. Or you could just poke yourself in the eye with a sharp stick and get it over with.

The decision isn't easy. On the one hand, you're driven by the need for companionship — another thing that separates us from such mammals as coyotes. A male coyote doesn't look for someone to beat at scrabble in front of a warm fire. He looks for someone to sniff and hump. And he doesn't take it personally if the female coyote grunts and runs. He moves on to the next "coyotease" until he finds one that holds still while she pleads, "Just don't knock me into that cactus, cowboy." This is why coyotes are always howling.

On the other hand, you're also driven by the need to be left alone. You're sick and tired of motivational speakers telling you to seize the day and swim with the sharks. You'd rather stay home and seize yourself.

Tossed between a rock and a hard place, or between getting your rocks off and a hard-on, you decide to try dating, which is why you need protection — and we're not talking about con-

It's a jungle out there.

doms. After all, it's a jungle out there, and condoms can't protect you from the worst danger of the jungle: LOVE — unless you wear a big one on your head!

· ·

**You're sick and tired of motivational speakers
telling you to swim with the sharks and seize the day.
You'd rather stay home and seize yourself.**

· ·

The wild dangers of the dating jungle scare you. You could get eaten. So then you think, "Hey...maybe the jungle isn't so bad." But in dating you could get heartbroken, a rash, herpes, or even worse, you could get...*married!*

Aside from these possible hurts, dating is a picnic. And if you can protect yourself from these dangers, dating can be fun for the whole family — as long as you don't date members of your family.

Dating Insurance

Your first line of protection is dating insurance. Many people think nothing of insuring themselves against fires, theft, floods, droughts, cyclones, tsunamis, accidents, sickness, death, or, God forbid, tartar buildup. But the biggest calamities are caused by relationships.

Think about it. If your car gets stolen, you know who to call. If your wallet gets stolen, you know who to call. But if your man or woman gets stolen, who are you going to call? Ghostbusters? Insurance doesn't cover those liabilities — until now.

Our research has discovered a new company that is about to come on the scene called AllDate Insurance. AllDate Insurance will insure you against any and all possible damages resulting from dating. All the policies will be on a no-fault basis, because everyone always thinks it's the other person's fault. Naturally, chronic cheaters, losers, and boozers will get put in the assigned risk category. Men's policies will be more expensive because they're much more reckless where they park their cars. AllDate Insurance will become very sensitive to hurt because these claims will hurt them plenty.

The claims will fall into three major categories:

- financial damages—when you lose your money.
- physical damages—when you lose your health.
- psychological damages—when you lose your mind.

The policies will cover such things as: getting stood up, getting shot down, shooting up, getting shot at, and accidentally impaling your date with a cocktail fork.

THE PRE-DATING CONTRACT

The pre-dating contract is an essential ingredient of dating protection. Not only does it reduce the likelihood of a post-date law suit, it also clarifies intentions and reduces misunderstandings, such as whether there was any interest to begin with.

Below is a sample contract. It should be reviewed by your attorney and signed before starting the date. If you are dating your attorney, sue your attorney. If you can still get along, the two of you might be soul mates.

PRE-DATING CONTRACT

This agreement is made between _Brenda Cornhoggle_ hereafter known as GOLD DIGGING DITZ [DITZ], and living at _134 Princess Court_ , hereafter known as SAFE HAVEN. And _Hiram Fitz-puddle_ , hereafter known as MACHO PIG [PIG] and living at _54 Coppafeel Rd._ , hereafter referred to as HUMP HEAVEN and collectively referred to as the THE-SOON-TO-BE-DISAPPOINTED (a.k.a. PLAINTIFF AND DEFENDANT).

Term of Date

Date will occur on _Friday the 13th_ and begin at _7:35 P.M._ and end at approximately _1:25 AM_ . I understand that if DITZ follows The Rules and ends date early, DITZ will be required to pay for all date expenses. If PIG extends date without prior written consent, he will have to finance DITZ's three-day shopping spree.

Activity

PIG AND DITZ agree to perform the following dating activity, hereby referred to as THE EVENT. _Go to Ned's Car Wash and Bar and Girl for Monday Night Mudwrestling and Live Frog Eating Contest_

Payment of expenses

PIG agrees to be liable for the following expenses. All other expenses not listed shall be the direct responsibility of DITZ:
• Change for dinner from vending machine.

- Up to six pitchers of beer.
- DITZ's transportation from EVENT to Emergency Room for throwing up from beer.

Medical Evaluation

PIG AND DITZ hereby confirm they have had a comprehensive medical examination within the past six months, and that they are free from viruses, herpes, STD'S (sexually transmitted diseases), STC's (sexually transmitted cooties), split skull from tossed hand ax, finger nails with sharp scratchy edges, or a lot of credit card debt.

Psychiatric Evaluation

PIG AND DITZ hereby confirm they are of sound mind, aside from the insanity of dating each other. They further assert they are free of multiple personality disorders, but that the personality they do have needs a lot of work. Furthermore, neither is catatonic, schizophrenic, psychotic, neurotic, bulimic, or sarcastic.

Conversation

Neither of the SOON-TO-BE-DISAPPOINTEDS shall monopolize more than 99% of the conversation. For the one with the 1%, conversation shall be limited to: "House dressing will be fine, but could you put it on the side."

Sexual Activity

Should any sexual activity occur, such activity will be between two consenting adults — even though they are acting like children. Furthermore, all sexual activity shall be limited to (check one):
☐ Sweet kiss goodnight
☐ Sweet kiss good morning

- ☐ Petting in the car
- ☐ Petting in the zoo
- ☐ Petty larceny
- ☐ Holding each other while watching the moon
- ☐ Mooning each other while being put on hold
- ☐ Doing the nasty
- ☐ Nothing at all — each party can take matters into their own hands when returning home

Accidental Sexual Activity Clause

PIG and DITZ are hereafter indemnified and held harmless as a result of accidental sexual activity. Such activity shall include, though not be limited to:

- ☐ Accidental <u>gazing</u> upon the breast
- ☐ Accidental <u>grazing</u> upon the breast
- ☐ During movie, missing popcorn and reaching for nipple
- ☐ When looking for dropped contact lens under tablecloth, accidentally performing oral sex
- ☐ When walking together, accidentally tripping on sidewalk, landing in vagina

====

Protection From STD's: Sexually Transmitted Diseases

Many people think that the best protection from STD's is a condom. This is wrong. While condoms are important, clearly the best contraceptive is a crummy personality.

It's true. All a guy has to hear is some feminazi talk on and on about her boundaries, her standards, and her rights as a woman, and it will be impossible for him to crank up the love crane. It would be like trying to shoot pool with a rope. While she probably has many valid points, a good place to bring them up would be on *CNN's Crossfire,* not on a date. *Crossfire* would have her back. The date would leave skid marks.

On the other hand, a guy's self-serving *insistence* on sex is a turn-off. It turns off the very thing he wants to turn on — her sex guilt. If she wanted to be taken advantage of, she wouldn't be on a date. She would be getting a job as a White House intern.

The Condom Debate

Men don't like condoms. They claim it's like eating a gourmet meal with a sock on your tongue. While we're not putting down condoms, we're also not picking them up. Condoms can rupture, fall off, and cause coitus interruptus, another name for a lousy fucking break!

Yes, sex can kill you, but what can you do? Most things that give you pleasure can eventually kill you, such as living a long time or eating a lot of cheese.

Your only fool-proof method is to douse yourself with antiseptic, then wear a wet suit under a space suit, and do the horizontal polka in a pool of acid strong enough to kill any living organism, including you. Your other choice is to only sleep with

Unsafe sex

people who have never had sex before. So you can't even have sex with yourself unless you're a virgin.

They say when you sleep with someone, you sleep with everyone they've ever slept with. So before you have sex, ask yourself: "Is this someone I want to pass the entire Hell's Angels' DNA to?"

....

Men don't like condoms. They claim it's like eating a gourmet meal with a sock on your tongue.

....

Protection From Hurt: How To Avoid Intimacy

Most people avoid relationships to avoid getting hurt. That's why it is important to avoid intimacy. All that close sharing and deep caring may work for Dr. Zhivago, but after you've been burnt too many times, you're ready for Dr. Kevorkian.

Here are just a few tried-and-true ways to avoid intimacy, besides the obvious one of smearing yourself with raw sewage and parading naked in Times Square, singing "The Star Spangled Banner."

1. **Talk your head off.** Keep blabbing. Yadda yadda yadda. No one can hurt you if they can't talk to you. Use run-on sentences and stream-of-conscious associations. Only inhale when no one is looking.

2. **Criticize everything.** Distance yourself by being on the attack. Hey, it works in war, why not try it in love, since all is fair in love and war. Also use war cliches like that one. No matter what they say, respond with, "It's a long way to Tipperary." (See How to Criticize Your Partner for Practically Everything, page 80.)

3. **Be controlling.** Control them so they don't control you. Say things like, "If you want the *highway to the thigh way,* do it my way." Say "no" to any activity you don't initiate. If they ask why, become their parents. Say, "Because I said so. Now go to your room."

4. **Be defensive.** Never admit you are wrong. Whatever happened, *they* did it. Blame them for everything. Start with the lights they left on and the water they left running. Progress to the fighting in the Mideast and global warming. Continue to the disappearance of the dinosaurs. Remember, it's *their* fault!

5. **Instead of a human being, become a human doing.** Always keep something fidgety going. Take calls in the middle of sex. Make calls in the middle of sex. Be a doer.

6. **Be late.** Late for anything — it doesn't matter. No one can get to you if you haven't shown up yet. Then, as soon as you arrive, say, "Ooops! Gotta go. I'm late."

7. **Be a control freak. Do all six together.** When combined, these methods create an impenetrable wall. Even Red Chinese torturers couldn't break through. First, the torturers couldn't ask you to talk because *you'd never shut up!* If they did scream in your face, you'd criticize their bad breath and disgusting manners. Whatever they asked you, you'd counter by saying, "None of your business, now go to your room." Then explain you are busy and don't have time to answer these stupid questions. Besides, *you're late!* The Beijing Macy's closes in half an hour. Finally, be defensive. Say, *"I've* got nothing to hide, what are *you* trying to hide, Chung Ho?"

Using the Mafia for Protection

In dating you can never have too much protection. That's why you should take advantage of any mafia connections you have in

I always carry protection on a date, Fred.

any part of the world. If your uncle's third cousin is Luigi the Weasel, invite him on the date as a chaperone. If you're a guy and your woman doesn't put out, have Luigi break her kneecaps. If you're a woman and your guy has his hands all over you like an octopus, have Luigi break his kneecaps.

Once you feel protected, you are ready for the next stage in dating: OBSESSION. You can go through this stage with confidence knowing you are completely safe. Sadly, it's your *partner* who is in great danger. You will know you have entered this stage because you get the *hots*.

3

Obsession
When you get the hots

Well, you've bit the bullet, swallowed your pride, donned a stiff upper lip, and now you are ready for — a stiff drink, which will give you the guts to pop enough Valium, Prozac, and tiny time capsules to get out there and date. And the first person you might date is the doctor in the emergency room pumping your stomach, but it's a start. No time to be picky. Hospitals are great places to meet lonely and desperate people.

Note: They're not good places to meet party animals. Party animals don't hang around hospitals looking for a good time. They're usually rushed to the hospital *because* they had a good time.

But sadly, Mr. or Ms. Right is not going to find you. They're not going to scale the fire escape and jimmy open your window wearing a tuxedo or strapless gown asking if you'd like your martini shaken or stirred. It doesn't happen. And even if it did happen, you know damn well they're not Mr. or Ms. Right because they would have known you wanted a Banana Daiquiri.

That's why you have to go out and find them.

Getting Out of the House

So it's time to get out of the house and be creative. Every location is a possible "meet" market, even the road. A turnpike can become a singles' party, and the tolls are the cover charge. Drive with a bumper sticker saying: HONK IF YOU'RE HORNY. It will get drivers to pull down their windows, and who knows what else they'll pull down.

As you drive, look to your left — Mr. Right might be there. If he's not, it could be Mr. Alright-for-Now. Look to your right — it may not be the love of your life but, hey, it could be the love of your night. *There's got to be somebody somewhere you haven't pissed off yet.* Get a date. Anyhow, anywhere, anyone — just get one.

If you are a woman, remember: men are like dogs. When dogs see another dog peeing, they want to pee there too. If a man sees you dating, he'll also want to date you — or pee on you. So get a date with someone — anyone.

••

**There's got to be somebody somewhere
you haven't pissed off yet.**

••••••••••••••••••••••••••••••••••

If you are a man, remember that women are different. They are not generally attracted to a man who plays the field. Women like a man who is heartbroken, so walk around with a sad look on your face. If you're introduced to a prospective girlfriend, say, "Oh, a woman." Then cower in fear like an abused puppy who's been struck with a rolled newspaper. They'll know you've had your heart ripped out. They'll want to cradle you in their arms and take you home to rescue you from the pound. They'll want to mend your little puppy heart so they can rip it out and stomp on it in their own special way. Just don't pee on them.

But sometimes you don't want to meet just anyone. You want to meet your one and only, your be-all-and-end-all, your better half, the yang to your yin, the slam to your bam, the flip to your flop — your soul mate. There's just one question you need to answer: WHAT THE HELL IS A SOUL MATE?

In Search of a Soul Mate

Let's face it; even Leonard Nimoy is going to pass on this one. He'll search for Atlantis, the secret to Stonehenge, and the mystery behind the fad of Beanie Babies, but a soul mate? Forget it. No one knows, though everyone *thinks* they know.

Everyone *thinks* your soul mate is the person you are destined to be with — the person who will make your life complete. Magically, they know what you want and need, and when you find them, your pimples will finally clear up.

After only a few months, and more often a few hours, you realize they're just what the doctor ordered — a pill! The truth is, your soul mate can set you off faster then a code red at a trauma center. They'll work your last nerve like a crying baby on a transglobal flight. The only thing they'll *really* share with you is a communicable disease. And after the relationship is over, they'll knife you in the back and then have you arrested for carrying a concealed weapon!

Because people are preoccupied with this deranged image of their soul mate, perfectly good lovers go by the wayside — just because they never read *The Celestine Prophesy*. So don't rule anyone out.

••

After the relationship is over, your soul mate will knife you in the back and then have you arrested for carrying a concealed weapon!

••

She listens to Tupac Shakur, he reads Deepak Chopra — close enough! He wears Gucci, she loves Lucy — no worry. She drinks wheat grass, he'd rather pass gas — there's hope. The important mantra to remember is that anybody is better than nobody, providing they're better than nothing at all.

If you are lucky enough to find a soul mate, just hope they're of the same species. That's because some people claim their pet is their soul mate. The one advantage of an inter-species relationship is that you don't have to be faithful. If you're in love with your gerbil, it won't be jealous if you're petting the cat on the side.

New Places to Meet Your Soul Mate

Now that you haven't a clue as to what or who your soul mate is, naturally you can't wait to meet them. Here are a few places we suggest you try:

1. **Have an operation you don't need.** There are plenty of single anesthesiologists. These are the organs you can afford to lose: spleen, one kidney, appendix, gall bladder, tonsils, uterus, part of your colon, a testicle, a breast, and some skin.

2. **A House of God.** Convert to a strange religion every week. After all, your spirituality means nothing if you're not getting laid.

3. **Funerals.** Read the obits and go to the funerals of widows and widowers. You know there's at least one single person there.

4. **Lemaze classes.** For men, what's better than a room full of women doing heavy breathing?

5. **Sex Addicts Anonymous meetings.** At least you'll know your soul mate isn't a prude. Offer to keep having sex until they can finally cut down.

6. **Court arraignments.** Your potential spouse may be going to prison, but at least you know they can wear horizontal stripes.

7. **Buy a car.** People will talk to a car before they talk to a person.

8. **Buy a dog.** People will talk to a dog before they talk to a car.

That's him. That's my soul mate.

9. **Get involved in a war.** The front lines are filled with desperate men and women.

10. **Your cable installation.** These men and women are seriously pre-screened by the cable companies, and you could get free HBO!

11. **Call 911.** When the rescuers come, clasp your heart and say, "Oh, I'm so alone."

12. **A natural disaster.** You never know when your soul mate will come floating by during a flood.

13. **Braille classes.** Blind people make great lovers. They may be touchy, but they're not picky.

14. **A gay bar.** Even if you're straight. You never know who's really gay and who's just confused.

15. **A straight bar.** Even if you're gay. Straight people experiment all the time.

16. **Your home.** After you get to a certain age, you just can't afford to discount family members.

17. **Climb Mt. Everest without oxygen.** Someone will have to come give you mouth-to-mouth.

18. **Interrupt any conversation around you.** Just butt in by saying, "That's a lie." Then introduce yourself.

19. **Take a voodoo class.** Stick a pin in a random voodoo doll and look around and see who clasps their heart. That's your soul mate. You can tell them so on the way to the hospital.

20. **A car accident.** Don't be afraid to ram someone you are attracted to. It's a great icebreaker.

21. **Go to a third world country.** You can pick someone up there *cheap.*

**Pretend you're choking. Whoever performs
the Heimlich maneuver might be your soul mate.**

THE PERSONAL AD

Another way to find your soul mate is to have your soul mate find you. This is done through the personal ad. The sad truth is love is a business, and very few businesses can survive without advertising. Even sadder is that you are the product of the business, and your shelf life is expiring. Yes, you are a carton of milk and you are about to go sour — a carton of milk with a picture of your lost inner child on the side pleading to be found.

So it's time to advertise. Put the word out. Write a personal ad. Make a flyer and wallpaper the town. Start a multi-level marketing scheme. Make love your business. That's right, make your business monkey business. After all, what you do with your business is no one else's business.

Writing the perfect personal ad is a skill, however, and below are a few "do's and don't's" to get you started:

Bad Personal Ads

"Reward money offered to anyone responding to this ad."

"Seeking someone seeking me."

"Call me. I won't hurt you. Not at first, anyway."

Good Personal Ads

"Love goddess seeking her Adonis. I'm naked, always."

"Brains, beauty, and brawn, that's me. If you are same, call. No losers need apply. I may be shallow, but I can afford to be — I'm rich too."

"Over-protective maternal type looking for boy toy. Call me. I'll let you wet my bed."

**European gentleman with striking appearance
and active nightlife seeks night person for
long term relationship. Type "O" blood a plus.**

Translating Classified Ad Terminology

Sometimes the terminology in personal ads is obvious, like the following one:

SWM sks Nkd Wmn 2 Eat

Other times it's not so obvious, and you need the help of this survival guide to understand what the other person is saying. For example:

DSW sks WPM tBT&PC

means "Desperately suicidal woman seeks wealthy paternal mogul to bankroll therapy and prozac costs."

and:

HDM sks HSF r/h S th Sp

means "Horny dominant male seeks horny submissive female who would rather have sex than shop."

How to Initiate a Call

The best way to give someone your phone number is by handing it to them. Most phone numbers are seven digits. If you ask someone for their number and the paper reads 222-33, you've probably been had — unless they live in Antarctica, where they don't use phones. They just tap on the ice in Morse Code. In Antarctica "222-33" is Morse Code for "I'm frickin' freezing," so rip up the number. They're geographically undesirable. Of course, if the number is 1-800-PISSOFF, a man shouldn't bother dialing it. She's not interested.

What Do Women Want?

What a woman wants depends on the day you ask her. Most women want a man who wants a woman. Women also want a man who wants *them*. They also want a man who wants them the *way* they want them to want them. And they also want a man who wants what *they* want. In other words, a woman wants a...*woman!*

But when a woman pictures her ideal man, this is how her pictures stack up in importance:

1. **A Hollywood movie star, rock star, or sports star.** Most women would not think twice about jumping the bones of a Hollywood star. You can be sure they're not going to say, "Titanic, Schmitanic, Leonardo DiCaprio, I don't go down on the first date." In a New York minute they'll be pelvis-loose and panty-free.

2. **A cultural or local hero.** These men may swim in a small pond, but in their world they're a big fish. We're talking about Scott, the school quarterback; Bruiser, the leader of the biker gang; or Freddy, lead singer of Freddy and the Frenetics. Many women think they're cool — even though they could use an ego-ectomy.

3. **Any success object.** While men get turned on by sex objects, women get turned on by success objects. If a woman is staring at a bulge in a guy's pants, she's hoping it's his wallet. Some women go for Ed, President of Cyberspace Intercellular Systems. Others go for Hyram, head surgeon for Bankruptyou Hospital. As long as their credit cards are platinum, these guys are gold.

> **You can be sure they're not going to say, "Titanic, Schmitanic, Leonardo DiCaprio, I don't go down on the first date.**

4. **A fun meister.** Yes, believe it or not, girls just want to have fu-hun. This guy owns nothing, but he's a laugh-a-minute. He's so much fun, he makes the time whiz by when she's passing the hat. But if he ever runs out of material, she'll run out on him.

Women are sex objects. Men are success objects.

5. **Good looks and a tight end.** Women like guys with cute buns, so if his beer belly grows to that of a Sumo wrestler, he should get a "tushie-tuck."

What Do Men Want?

Men want whatever women don't want. When men were asked if they thought they'd ever find the perfect person, they said, "If I ever get enough cash." Behind closed doors men's number one want is a gorgeous woman. They don't even care if *they* are attracted, as long as their friends and business associates are attracted.

Yes, men do like boobs. Fortunately, God didn't give them any, otherwise they wouldn't want women at all.

WHAT MEN AND WOMEN *SAY* THEY WANT AND WHAT THEY *REALLY* WANT

What She Says She Wants	What She Really Wants
Someone who understands me.	Someone who understands how much money I need.
Someone strong, handsome, and smart.	Someone obviously already taken.
Someone honest and caring.	A rich man who honestly doesn't care if I do nothing.
Someone sensitive and sweet.	Sensitive to my feelings. Screw his.
A soul mate.	I don't need one. I have my cat.

What He Says He Wants	What He Really Wants
An attractive woman	Boobs so big my friends are drooling. And I don't care what she had to do to get them.
A pleasing personality	Someone who does what I say.
A smart woman	Someone who is smart enough to shut up and do what I say.
A soul mate	Someone who is smart enough to shut up and do what I say — with big boobs.

MEN AND WOMEN APPROACH DATING DIFFERENTLY

Because men and women are different, each needs a different approach to making each other miserable. Simply put, men collect as many numbers as possible that they won't call, while women get as many men attracted to them that they can ignore. In other words men use modern sales and telemarketing techniques while women play hard to get.

Men Use Modern Sales and Telemarketing Techniques

Men are often cold and calculating. They realize that relationships are business — usually a business loss, but business nevertheless. A man has to treat the dating process as a business of sales, and sales is a numbers game. If you get shot down, so what. In baseball if you screw up 70% of the time, you're batting .300 and you could get into the Hall of Fame. That's why men need to learn the fine art of telemarketing. Here are the steps:

1. Get leads.

Any good salesman works with leads. The better the lead, the better the chance of a sale. Sales are dates. Dates are sex. Sex is good. Therefore, *leads equals sex* (ipso logica defacto).

Leads can be gotten anywhere — classified ads, singles events, riots, floods, voices in your head. This is no time to be a snob.

2. Work the phone.

If you get a number, call it promptly. Be a premature communicator. Women respond to enthusiasm, but not too much enthusiasm. You don't want to come across like a Harrier jump-jet waiting to dock on the U.S.S. Vagina.

3. Schedule dates.

Any good salesman knows that you don't go for the sale over the phone. Schedule an appointment. Women call this a date. Men call it a business meeting where, if you close the deal, you may end up naked. All men would like to have sex on the first date, but this is a bad plan. Instead of giving the shaft, he'll usually get the shaft.

Hi, Jane, great timing. Could you hold a minute? Alice, could you hold for a second? Judy, what's happening? Hold on, I'll be right with you. Betty? Hold on. Martha? Hold on. Liz? Hold...

4. Follow through.

Follow-through is critical. Keep a rotating index card file. If she can't make it one night, call her back for another. As the names of women mount in the hundreds, get a personal secretary to handle the calls and correspondence. Then date the secretary.

5. Maximize your sales with the computer.

Since date books are now outdated, the modern man needs a computer to track his successes and failures.

Record the details of every date with DATADATE 3.0 to avoid reminiscing about a concert you suddenly realize you went to with someone else. If you need to pretend you saw a movie as an alibi, log on to FAKEAMOVIE.COM. If you are a compulsive voyeur, get PEEPING TOM for Windows 5.1. To manage your dating finances, get QUICKIE 6.9. And, finally, get MIND YOUR OWN BANKRUPTCY 2.1 since you must now quit your job and attend your social life full time.

••

Men collect as many numbers as possible that they won't call, while women get as many men attracted to them that they can ignore.

••

Women Play Hard to Get by Following A Stupid Book Called *The Rules*

The Rules says that playing hard to get works — that if a woman can dangle her love box a few inches beyond a man's reach, he'll follow her anywhere. It's the carrot-on-the-stick technique. It often works because a guy's carrot can't hold a stick to the effect her love box has on his dangle. This can backfire because *when a woman keeps playing hard to get, she becomes very easy to forget.*

The premise of *The Rules* is that a man needs a challenge — that he is a dragon slayer looking for a dragon. As if getting out of bed in the morning wasn't a big enough challenge. *The Rules* doesn't acknowledge that today's women also love a challenge. Of course, many of today's women are *men*.

••

**When a woman keeps playing hard to get,
she becomes very easy to forget.**

••

Nevertheless, women keep playing games, following prescribed, fixed, rigid rules that make them as spontaneous and fun to be with as the head clerk at the motor vehicle bureau. The key rule in following *The Rules* is that you treat men you are interested in like men you are not interested in. And who can refute the wisdom of this approach? There's no greater turn-on for a man than being treated like he's not wanted. Every man likes to be hung up on, ignored, rejected, and cussed out. It's also good to belittle a man, especially if his penis is little. This generates interest and fuels a man's fire. And, of course, if you want him to be yours forever, spray Mace in his face and get an order of protection against him. In no time at all you'll be hearing wedding bells, though they might be drowned out by the sirens of the police investigating your sudden disappearance.

Women Taking the Risk: Initiating a Call to a Guy

All right, you're a woman and you decide to take the bull by the horns. In fact, you're tired of the bull and you're starting to get horny. The trouble is that on the planet Bras, the only man you know how to call is your mechanic. So the call may go something like this:

Hello, it's me, with the red convertible. I thought maybe you'd like to check my oil and rotate my tires.

or:

Hello, grease monkey? My engine is overheating. Could you put me up on your lift and look under my hood? I need my tubes lubed and my gears smeared.

What to Do if He Doesn't Call

Okay, so the cute guy with no dangling nose hairs at the wedding asked you for your number. You danced cheek-to-cheek all night, and you've decided that this man is definitely someone you want your kids spending every other weekend with — BUT he never calls!

••

Innuendo is protected by the First Amendment. Actually, the First Amendment doesn't mention innuendo specifically, but it does allude to it indirectly.

••

What can you do? NOTHING. Move on with your life. If you do choose to sit around and wait for the phone to ring, find a secondary hobby — like knitting a life-size replica of the Eiffel Tower out of steel wool, something to keep you busy. Whatever you do, don't you call him either!!! Pretty soon no one will be calling anyone, and even though your heart is broken, at least you showed him! And you can use the Eiffel Tower as a tourist attraction.

HOW TO FLIRT

Flirting is an art; it takes practice. The more you practice, the better you get. Practice on anything. Walk up to a fish tank and wink at a guppy. Just make sure it's the opposite sex — fish are notoriously homophobic. Leer at a plant; see if it grows. Ogle a tree; if it doesn't leave, you're good. Practice — on anything!

But you can't flirt with a conscience. This is war, so take no prisoners; flirt anywhere. If you're a man, be a dude that's crude, rude, and lewd. Find a woman at the Post Office and say, "I'd like to lick your stamps." Create! See a girl in a parking lot and ask,

"Can I park my car in *your* space?" Walk up to a woman at a fruit stand and say, "Mind if I squeeze your mangoes?" *You can turn any ordinary remark into a tactless sexual innuendo.* And they can't sue you because innuendo is protected by the First Amendment. Actually, the First Amendment doesn't mention innuendo specifically, but it does allude to it indirectly.

Women Are More Subtle When They Flirt

Women are masters of the elusive suggestive turn-on. They are so good most men don't have a clue the woman is actually flirting. To help a man tune in to a woman's signals, here's an exercise he can do:

> **Exercise for men:** Put on a dress and look at yourself in the mirror in such a coy way that you are pretending not to be interested in yourself.

Six Ways a Woman Can Flirt

Women, now that men are starting to read your body language — or negotiate your curves — **here are a few ideas to help you flirt:**

1. Smile, make eye contact for about three to five seconds in a way that says, "I can't pay my bills."

2. Look at him with your eyes saying, "If you're interested, I don't bite, that is unless *you're* into it."

3. Casually touch his hand while talking. If he doesn't respond, drip hot wax on his knuckles that spells out HELP ME!

4. Ask him to carry something for you into your house. When he gets inside, bolt the doors and weep.

5. Make eye contact; then slowly drop your eyes to your breasts and say, "Life is a mountain climb and that's your Matterhorn."

6. Nod at him from across the room, wink, lick your lips, and mouth the words, "I need dental work done."

Chicks like to be lured in with a good line, Ralph.

Pickup Lines

You can get someone's interest by using a little ingenuity in your introduction. This is done with the pickup line. "Hi, how are you?" is not only dull, no one gives a damn how you are. You can pique someone's interest right away with the well-picked pickup line.

These are some good pickup lines for men and women:

- Care for a spanking?

- I'm such a woman, I go through a bra a day.

- Wanna hold my beer while I take a wicked piss?

- Hi. If you ever need anybody's legs broken, let me know.

- My body's a temple and every night I pray to God someone enters it.

- I've been following you for five years. God, you walk fast.

- Could you hold still while I take your temperature?

- I lost my puppy. Please help me find him. I think he went into that cheap motel.

Some bad pick up lines:

- How do you like your eggs?

- I'd like to buy you a drink. Could you loan me ten bucks?

- I have a note from my urologist. I'm not contagious any-more.

- I'm old fashioned. I like a man to take me out to dinner before I sue him.

- That's not a pickle in my pocket, it's a gun.

- Hey, nice breasts! Are they paid for?

- Grab their genitals and say, "It's okay; I'm a Doctor."

The Reverse Pickup

Most men resent coughing up heavy dough for three or four dates just to find out the woman he is dating has the wrong chemistry, or that she has something he's not looking for — like a penis. He would prefer knowing things like this a little sooner. That's why he should try the reverse pick up.

The normal pickup is:

1. A man meets a woman in a bar and introduces himself. The conversation is awkward because each is trying to impress the other while appearing aloof.

2. He buys her drinks and as the conversation starts lightening up, so does his wallet.

3. He now suggests dinner. If he picks Burger King, he's ham-burger. So he picks Le Stuque Uppe Ristorante, mentally preparing to ask MasterCard if they take American Express.

4.   Then he suggests a visit to his place for some phony reason — to help him decipher the hieroglyphics on his Rosetta Stone. She says she'd love to, but she has to get up early for work. Her ego's boosted. His ego's busted.

The reverse pick-up is much more effective:

1.   You meet a babe in a bar and you suggest some hot steamy kinky sex. If she doesn't screw you — screw her! If she says, "yes," Ta da! You're doing the horizontal boogaloo and you feel there just might be a God after all. And now, since you've worked up an appetite....

2.   It's time to go for dinner. If you're a cheapass trailer trash, you'll take her to a 7-11 and order some pork rinds with a side of motor oil. But now you should celebrate — go for the full monty. Take her to a place the health inspectors haven't boarded up yet. The hell with your debt. MasterCard can Discover it can use its Visa to book a one-way trip straight to hell. And, of course...

3.   It's time for drinks. Yes, it's champagne with the ostentatious bucket that makes everyone ask, "Who are those assholes trying to impress, anyway?" And now it's getting late. Be sensitive; say, "Don't you have to get up early for work?" So you take her home and just before you say goodnight...

4.   You ask her name and introduce yourself.

Stroking the Male Ego

The quickest way to a man's heart is to continually tell him lies about himself which he eventually believes. This gives him a warm feeling. Men even say that what they fall in love with is the way a woman makes them *feel*. They fall in love with a feeling — about *themselves*. Women just happen to be passing through at the time. Talk about narcissists! Women, on the other hand, fall in love with the *man*. So most happy couples have one huge thing in common — they both love *him!*

....

**Men fall in love with a feeling —
about *themselves*. Women just happen
to be passing through at the time.**

....

Flattering the Opposite Sex:
Avoiding Back-Handed Compliments

Flattery will get you everywhere in dating, but sometimes even the most sincere compliments can backfire. For example:

RIGHT: You look fabulous.
WRONG: You've lost weight, but don't get me wrong; you didn't look bad fat, either.

**Morris, you've got to stop buying hair
from the Home Shopping Network.**

RIGHT: That outfit makes you look so young and playful.
WRONG: You look good for someone over the hill.

RIGHT: I love your hair.
WRONG: Your toupee works beautifully with the hair weave. You really don't need to use the spray paint.

How to Turn Flirting in the Workplace Into a Sexual Harassment Lawsuit

There was a time when flirting was legal. You could actually ask someone out in the workplace without your lawyer present. Now if you ask someone out at work, you can be sure they're wearing a "wire" while a hidden camera records the interaction for a class-action law suit. And that's if the person is *interested* in you.

If you want to ask out someone you work with, your best bet is to fire them first. Here's how that conversation might go:

Hi Betty, it's Mr. Morgan. I have good news and I have bad news. The bad news is you're fired. The good news is that since you have all that free time, I've booked us both on a five-day cruise to the Bahamas.

Even if the other person isn't asking you out, you can still persuade a jury that you have been sexually harassed. **Innocent comments can easily be misconstrued in your favor. For example:**

- Can you grab my floppy disc?

- You've loaded my hard-drive.

- My assistant gives good phone and takes great dictation.

- I'm not used to having such a smart man under me.

- I like my coffee like I like my women: strong, black, and one after another.

If you are the victim of sexual harassment, don't wait until the perpetrator runs for political office to file the suit. File your confession now .Then get a book and movie deal, pose for *Playboy,* sell out to *The National Enquirer,* and get a lecture tour — because if you give a confession without a lecture tour, you're just another Catholic.

How a Man Can Tell if He Has Been Shot Down.

Most men have egos the size of Moby's dick. They don't always know when they've been rejected. When they do, it feels like they've been kicked in the groin — which is why women aim for their groin. It's a lot more sensitive than they are.

....

**Most men have egos the size of Moby's dick...
which is why women aim for their groin.
It's a lot more sensitive than they are.**

....

Nevertheless, as we march into the new millennium, men are getting more tuned in to the hearts and minds of women. They can actually detect if they've been shot down, without having their nuts blown off by a surface-to-surface missile. **A man can tell if he's been shot down if a woman says any of the following:**

- Coffee, tea, or Mace?

- I wouldn't date you if you paid me — unless it was a huge amount.

- The FBI may want you, but I don't.

- You could buy me a hundred drinks, but you'd still be too ugly to sleep with.

- Here's a hand grenade. Could you hold it for me until I get back?

Signs that Your Dream Date Is About to Turn into a Nightmare.

If you've never been on a bad date, then you've never been on a date. Dating is worse than shucking oysters where every fourth one is rancid, twisted, shrunken and inedible. Unfortunately, dating doesn't enjoy the stellar track record of a shucked oyster.

But if you pay attention to subtle clues, you can reduce your dating disasters. For example, if a man says to you, "I'm not a nice guy." Don't say, "Yes you are," and think he's a fixer-upper. He's a prick and he just told you! And if a woman says, "I'm going to rip your heart out and pour acid on it," don't think, "She's honest! I love her." She's a bitch and she's planning to use your testicles as bait for a shark hunt in the South Pacific.

Clues the Man You Are About to Go Out With is not Normal

1.   He shows up with his mother.

2.   His beard is parted in the middle and he's nicknamed it "The Red Sea."

3.   He tells you he's a back-to-basics kind of guy and shows up with a horse and buggy.

4.   His nanny answers the door and says, "Make sure he takes his medicine every fifteen minutes."

5.   Instead of ringing your doorbell, he stands on the front step and yells, "Ding-dong."

6.   He rings your doorbell and when you ask who it is, he says, "The man that's going to kill you."

7.   His fly is undone and a mouse crawls out.

Clues the Woman You Are About To Take Out is not Normal

1. She doesn't remember you had a date.

2. The address she gave you is a 7-11, and she's standing in front reading *The Transexual Times*.

3. She answers the door in a wedding gown.

4. She says, "Let's split. I just dropped acid and I wanna be gone before the Genie knows I'm missing."

5. She's wearing a FREE CHARLIE MANSON button.

6. She's bleeding from her left side and says, "The operation was a success."

7. When you knock on her door, it creaks open like a horror movie, and her face is being eaten out by maggots.

Another first date ruined by a case of spontaneous combustion.

DATING ETIQUETTE
Do's and Dont's for Men

DO: Pick her up at her home like a gentleman.
DON'T: Set a paper bag of cow manure on fire, ring the bell, and run away.

DO: Open all doors, hold her chair, and help her off with her coat.
DON'T: Help her off with all her clothes — especially in a crowded restaurant.

DO: Let her order first — whatever she wants.
DON'T: Bug your eyes out of your sockets like Wiley Coyote when she orders the lobster, immediately suggesting the lettuce and tomato sandwich.

DO: Pay for everything for the first couple of dates.
DON'T: Ask her to cough up half of the dinner tab. This is tacky,

HOW TO TREAT A DATE

Wrong!   Right!

There. that's my half!

and at best will get you back 11 bucks, which barely covers the bag of cow manure you left on her porch. Besides, if you ask her to cough up for half the dinner, she may cough up something else, since women are known to be revengeful.

DO: Put her back where you found her at the end of the night.
DON'T: Curse at her when she tells you she doesn't believe in petting on the first date. Don't say, "I spent twenty-two dollars on you, you owe me, you cock teaser." The goodnight is up to her. If she offers you her hand, take it. If she offers you her breast, shake it.

Do's and Don't's for Women

DO: Be gracious if a man inadvertently fails to hold the door for you.
DON'T: Wait there like a wounded bird pointing out the man's flaws. Pointing out flaws to a man has the same effect as pouring ice water on his erection. Men don't like it. You've got two arms; open the damn door yourself!

DON'T: Offer him money on the first couple of dates.
DO: When the check comes, slip into the bathroom, slip into something more comfortable, slip into a coma — just slip into anything to avoid the wallet waltz and the dutch-treat tango.

DO: Lean over and unlock his door. This shows him you know how a car works. Men like smart chicks. It also proves you saw *A Bronx Tale.*
DON'T: Let him get drenched in the freezing rain while you sit like a stuck-up mannequin in the passenger seat. Help him out.

DO: When he takes you home, say "goodnight" and some encouraging words if you'd like to see him again.
DON'T: Invite him in to see your stamp collection and then really show him your stamp collection. If you invite a man in, he wants *IN!*

Playing the Field Without Stepping on a Mine

Maneuvering yourself around the dating field without a guide book is tricky. It's like a sperm trying to swim its way through a vasectomy. Each sex has different preferences.

Men hate dating because to them it's really just three hours in the way of sex. Men like to have sex on the first date mostly because they already know there's not going to be a second. Women do not like to have sex on the first date because they do not like taking their clothes off in front of strangers. On the planet Bras the body is fat and ugly. Even if you are a size four, you're fat. On Bras, at the birth of a chubby baby girl, the doctor doesn't spank, he induces vomiting.

On the other hand, men who are fat and ugly are brought up to love and flaunt their bulbous forms. These same men accuse their women of being fat. Many of them prance around in bikini bathing suits, grabbing their huge stomachs saying, "You know how many six-packs of Bud I've got here?"

**This Speedo is covering too much of me, honey.
Let's go to a nude beach.**

How to Break Up after the First Date

If you've decided this is the last date, there's a polite way of letting him or her know — LIE! At this stage you owe this person nothing, especially the truth. Just say, "This was fun, but tomorrow I must return to the Mother Ship."

The truth is something that should be reserved for very precious few people, such as a Grand Jury investigation, and even then it should be used sparingly. If you don't like to lie, try an honest, gentle comment like, "At the count of three, when I snap my fingers, we'll forget we ever met." If the person is foreign, you can always call immigration. They'll never suspect you and besides, guilt doesn't travel that far.

How to Break Up *before* the First Date

You were committed to going out with someone, but you've changed your mind. You're allowed to change your mind. That's another thing that separates us from other mammals — that and teenage acne. Other mammals don't buy Clearasil, and they don't go around changing their minds — they're too big. But you still have the right to be fickle. Fickledom is your unalienable right. Call them when you know they will be out, and leave the following message:

> "Hi, this is Penelope and I'm so looking forward to our date tonight. I really have a lot to be celebrating, too. The exorcism was a success. That's right, he's gone." *[Then lower your voice like the devil and continue:]* "That's what you think. You'll never get rid of me. I'll kill you first. And anybody who comes near you." *[Scream, then hang up.]*

You will never hear from this person again. We promise.

· ·

Women don't like sex on the first date because they don't like taking their clothes off in front of strangers.

· ·

The Second Date

On the second date ask for a dating resume with references that you call. Remember, no matter how incredible they seem, there is someone, somewhere who knows what an asshole they are. Find those people and make contact. Have lunch; start a softball team. And if possible, bring them together for a *Dateline* NBC exclusive undercover investigation. Men like ambitious women.

Remember, when he asks you out for a second date, do not shriek, "Ohmigod, you called! I just lost ten bucks." Just say, "Let me check my calendar," while you rustle some papers, pretending you're moving some dates around — even if you're only canceling an appointment to have your poodle's teeth flossed.

For men it is not presumptuous to ask for a urine specimen on the second date. In fact, this is the best way to find out if she has any taste. If she brings the specimen in a bag that matches her purse, she's got taste. If she hands you a baggy with a twist-tie, she's tackier than a velvet painting of Elvis. Ditch her.

···

**For men it is not presumptuous to ask
for a urine specimen on the second date.**

···

The Third Date

During the third date both parties are still on their best behavior. Awards should be given out for this level of acting such as, "Best performance by a needy heartbroken man pretending to be cool, confident, and full of cash."

I can't believe you haven't been snatched up, Harry.
Where have you been hiding all these years?

Things are loosening up a little bit, and it is OK to ask a few innocent questions, such as:

- What's with the handcuffs and leg irons?

- Who's that woman who keeps answering the phone when I call you? Because if there's one thing I hate in a man — it's his wife.

- Your Visa's not maxed, is it?

- Why do you have me drop you off at the State Mental Institution? Do you work there?

The general rule is, "Don't ask, don't tell." Denial is important. Let's face it, if it weren't for denial, our lives would be teeming masses of cancerous vomit. But thanks to the wonder of denial, everything's fine. And if someone accuses you of being in denial — deny it!

Denial Exercise

Close your eyes and repeat the following phrase:

For women

The sleezy, unemployed, unshaven bastard I am dating is not on parole. He is a gorgeous, rich, successful top-level agent in the FBI who visits the 83rd precinct every Thursday at 3PM to investigate police corruption.

For men

The whiny, nagging, haranguing malcontent that I think I am in love with is not a bitch. She's an actress researching the role of Lady MacBeth. The man she keeps spending the night with is also an actor and they're just rehearsing their lines.

Men try to Get to the Fourth and Fifth Dates as Quickly as Possible

Men have trouble negotiating what seems to be a never-ending gauntlet of dates before they have sex. It's the women who impose the "not 'til the fourth date" rule. That's why a man should try to schedule short, quick dates that are relatively inexpensive. For example:

1. Meet in the morning for a power breakfast.

2. Meet again for a power lunch.

3. Meet again for a power happy hour followed by a power dinner.

4. After dinner invite her back to your place for a power shower.

If she turns you down, get back on the telephone and invite your next prey to a power breakfast.

GETTING READY FOR SEX IN DATING

Sex in dating is a hot topic. But the topic can't be discussed properly without knowing your way around the various terms. And this means knowing your way around the bases.

The Bases In Dating

There is a lot of confusion about the bases in dating. And a lot of controversy. First, why is the woman's body cut up into a baseball diamond? Why isn't the male body partitioned for ring toss?

And why baseball? Football makes a lot more sense. After a guy does some hand maneuvers in the huddle, he throws a pass and, with any luck, carries his balls through the goal posts into the end zone. The fact that he immediately falls asleep is of no concern.

Nevertheless, baseball has been chosen as the official jargon of the World Dating Federation, so we're about to set the record straight. Here's why guys do a lot of swinging, hitting, and running around, only to find they're back in the "dug-house" after striking out.

Glossary of Terms

First Base. This means a guy has been able to successfully kiss a girl without getting his face slapped, his groin kicked, or his Johnson surgically removed with a sling blade. Getting to first base also means getting in with a woman's good graces — like getting her front-row seats to the sold-out Menudo Reunion. When this happens, the man is practically in her pants already.

Second Base. This term usually refers to petting above the waist. Of course we're referring to a woman, not a dog. Although, if she

Now class, who can find the pitcher's mound?

barks, growls, or wags her tail, he should be more concerned with getting rabies than getting laid.

Above the waist a woman has a lot of straps, clasps, and engineering going on. How much of this maze must a guy get through to claim second base? None of it. He just has to pet it without it biting back.

Most men claim a pet when it is actually a grope. When a man gropes to get to second, it's often the last base he gets before being tossed out of the game. If a woman has had more than three drinks, however, a man may be able to get further, but now we're talking wrestling, not baseball.

Second Base with a Long Lead. This is when a man reaches for certain mammary glands often worshipped by men from time immemorial — even if they are not real. Such soft succulent mounds of sensuous enticement have done more for the glamour industry than O.J. Simpson has done for Bruno Magli shoes. Should men ever caress them sensuously instead of turning their nipples into dials on a short-wave radio, women will be forever at their beck and call.

....

When a man gropes to get to second, it's often the last base he gets before being tossed out of the game.

....

Third base. Third base is below the waist — there is no getting around it, though God knows, men have tried. Men try to get around everything, which is why in the old days a woman used to wear a girdle. It kept the locks from jangling on her chastity belt. Now, between Mace, karate, and a restraining order, a woman has more ways of holding a man at bay. But if petting goes on below the waist, but above the knee caps, this is third base.

Third Base with a *Really* Long Lead. This is when a guy thinks he's got the woman in the palm of his hands. Depending on her agenda, however, she may actually have him by the balls. This stage is very important because if a guy can do some fancy footwork with his fingers, the gal can get off before the guy can get on. Unfortunately, this has only happened twice since World War II, and both times, beforehand, the gals had gone bareback riding for three hours.

Home Plate. 95% of history can be explained by a man's desire to get to home plate. The other 4% is his desire to disembowel a major country. The last 1% is his desire to consume beer and nachos while watching the Super Bowl.

Yes, getting to home plate is the be-all and end-all for men. But sometimes when a woman finds out how unsatisfying a man can be, she ends it all. After he does his slam and bam, he falls asleep before he can say, "Thank you m'am." This has given rise to the joke: "How can you tell if a woman had an orgasm?…The man wakes up."

The Bases in Dating for Women

For women going around the bases is a lot easier.

First Base.	Show up.
Second Base.	Show up alone.
Third Base.	Show up alive.
Home Plate.	Find a bed, kitchen table, or airplane restroom, preferably unoccupied.

Eight Ways that May Prevent a Woman from Scoring

If you're a woman, it's almost impossible for you not to score with a guy, unless you do any of the following:

1. Tell him you hope the quell bath worked.

2. Tell him you are really a man, but it's OK 'cause you're gay.

3. Tell him he's a lot more handsome than the doctors in the shock therapy ward.

4. Pull out a gun. Tell him if he makes love nice and easy, no one will get hurt.

5. When you explain you are a vegetarian, mention you still get occasional cravings for human flesh.

6. Tell him you are pregnant by Pretty Boy Bruno, the Mafia hit man.

7. Tell him you're free any night except the full moon when you'll be howling in the cemetery.

8. Tell him you'll have sex with him if he gives you one of his kidneys.

HAVING SEX

Having Sex for the First Time

Having sex for the first time with a new person is not always very good. Of course, for a man, even bad sex is good sex. For a woman, having sex for the first time is like eating snails for the first time. It appears exotic at first, but after the snail is lured out of the shell, it's not that good — unless the snail is soaked in butter and garlic. But you don't want to soak your date in butter and garlic — at least not until you've had sex for the third time.

First-time sex is often awkward. It's difficult to adjust to each other's habits and patterns. You find yourself saying things like, "You're very sexy, but the electric cattle prod is not doing a thing for my orgasm," and "It's not that I don't really love the deep tongue kissing, it's just that you're licking my liver."

It's best to let the man initiate sex; this way he feels like he's pulling something over on you. This is a big sport on the planet Penus. It gives Penusians the illusion they are in control. The big sport on the planet Bras is laughing that Penusians think they have *any control at all!*

So when is it okay to have sex? When sex will be better than okay. After all, it's not that hard to find someone who wants to have sex with you. The trick is finding someone who wants to have sex with you *again*.

But whatever you do, practice safe sex. Of course, these days even safe sex is risky. That's why we suggest you just stay home and use your vibrator to turn on your inflatable doll.

··

It's not that hard to find someone who wants to have sex with you. The trick is finding someone who wants to have sex with you *again*.

··

Casual Sex

Casual sex is a term that is often misunderstood. Some think it's the opposite of formal sex — black tie, white condom.

The truth is, no one knows what casual sex actually is. For a man, sex is anything but casual. "Obsessive-compulsive" is a lot more like it. "Casual" means relaxed, laid back, easygoing, nonchalant. This doesn't describe sex, it describes a game of "Go Fish."

An example of casual sex would be a businessman approaching a stranger saying, "Excuse me, madame. Do you have the time? And are you using your vagina? Could I borrow it for a few minutes?"

How to Tell if the Attraction Is Love or Just Sex

Some people fall in love with falling in love. Sometimes the falling in love part is fabulous, but everything else sucks. If you look at them and want to rip their clothes off on a beach, throw them on the sand, and ram them with your waves of love, that's probably not love, but a strong physical attraction.

On the other hand, if you want to pay their psychiatrist bills and clean their body hair from the clogged shower drain, it's most likely love.

The Wrong Response To "I Love You"

If you've become very intimate with someone and they tell you they have something to tell you, and what they have to tell you is that they have something to tell you, and they would like to tell you this something at the right time to be telling it, they might be trying to tell you something. Duh! — like maybe they love you.

....

**For a man, sex is anything but casual.
"Obsessive-compulsive" is a lot more like it.**

....

Even if the thought of somebody loving you is about as appealing as a coffee enema, help them out.
If they say, "I love you," don't say:

- Well that's gonna cost you.

- You make me sick.

- And you are?…

- That's your problem.

- Have your girl call my girl.

- Are you talkin' to me?

- I gotta pee.

Just say "thank you," and change the subject. If you have the creeps, then you probably don't feel the same way. If you don't feel like you want to vomit, give love a chance. It's a powerful virus — maybe you'll catch it.

Being In Love: Entering the Pit of Despair

There's no feeling like love. When they are falling in love, women want to shout it from the rooftops. They call everyone they know. They blab for hours about every detail of the relationship: "And then he looked in my eyes and said, 'I love you so much I won't let anybody hurt you except me.' " They can't stop talking about this love feeling. It feels like nothing else. It's kinda wet, wild, and scary — like water skiing over Niagara Falls.

Men respond differently. They enter the "pit of despair." They know they're going to be hooking up cable, lifting boxes, taking out her trash for the rest of their life, and watching *Sleepless In Seattle* on New Year's Eve. This pisses them off. They already miss their friends. And they hate that movie.

How to Tell if You Are with a Smother Lover

There are many people who crave intimacy a little too much. They recap their life in intimate excruciating detail. And then they quiz you on it. Their idea of oral sex is telling you about sex with past lovers.

Every minute they ask you what you're thinking. So be prepared, because "nothing" is the wrong answer. These people describe their bowel movements like sportscasters — up close and personal — just so you don't miss out on the full experience. Of course, they pee with the bathroom door open because *love means never having to say your're peeing.*

These people were breast-fed by their fathers. They are Vampires. They want to suck your *you* out of you and replace it with *them.*

Some indications you are with a smother lover are:

- When you fall asleep, she's staring at you.

- When you wake up, she's still staring at you.

- He makes you look inside his crevices with a flashlight.

- Then he makes you describe what you see.

- When you go out, she tries to read your mind by putting on your jock strap.

- When you go out, he tries on your underwear — just so he can be in your pants when you're not there.

....

**Love means never having
to say you're peeing.**

....

Stalking the One You Love

Although stalking is really annoying, illegal, and worst of all, not at all nice, it's still a sport that must be admired for its sheer craftsmanship.

Let's face it, if you had a chance to sneak a peek at your soon-to-be in their natural environs, you would; admit it! After all, God's looking over us all day, so God's a voyeur. Are you too good to spy? What are you saying then, that you're better than God? Talk about being conceited!

If someone came to you in a dark alley with pictures of your soon-to-be, you'd look, right? You're still a stalker, you just lack ambition. Or you're a closet stalker. You just don't have the gumption to get in your car and drive past their house for a drive-by snooping.

In that case stalk from the safety and comfort of your own home. Call them and then hang up to find out if they are home. If they're not, get the code to their answering machine and replay all their messages.

When you get the courage to break out of *your* house, break into *their* house. Move things so they know someone was there. Leave notes on their car. Sign them up for the cheese-of-the-month club. Go to their mother's house on holidays, bearing gifts.

When you find out their mother's maiden name, start using their credit cards. If you need guidance, rewatch *Fatal Attraction*.

Just remember that by stalking you exercise your First Amendment right to gather for any reason, including religious reasons. And your new religion? Voyeurism!

This obsession is about to wear off. You've found someone to love, but now you've changed your mind. You don't love them. You don't even like them. In fact, if you had a hammer, you'd hammer them in the morning. You're well on your way to hating your mate.

Now that the frog has turned into the prince, and the beast has turned into the prince, and Cinderella has reunited with the prince, very soon the police will be checking the crime scene for prints. You're about to enter the next stage of dating: REPULSION. This is when you get the *snots!*

4

Repulsion
When you get the snots

All good things must come to an end. But your relationship is not such a good thing, so it's not over — yet. You just wish it was.

Your love has turned. And when love turns, it turns fast and it turns bad. It's like cottage cheese. One day it's healthy protein and the next day it's rotting fungus with green shit all over it. Do not eat love that's gone bad.

Indications You May Have Moved in Too Soon

You were a hopeless romantic and you decided that you must be joined at the hip. So you moved in together. You'd only known each other five days, but this was the real thing. You were a love tornado — blowing away anything that might get in the way of being together — like the fact that the two of you had nothing in common. **Some indications you moved in too soon are:**

- Her husband is still packing.

- When you tell people, they say, "Are you out of your fricking mind?"

- When you asked him to move in, he said, "It sounds like a good idea, but I don't know where you live."

- She still hasn't plastered the bullet holes from her last relationship.

Things That Used to Be Cute Now Annoy the Living Crap out of You

Yes, your love is receding fast. It's receding faster than the rain forest. **Things that used to be adorable now are deplorable:**

Men

- She has 50 pairs of shoes and she names them after the states of the union.

- After sex she yells out, "Thank God that's over."

- She has nipple hair.

- At night she puts her nipple hair in curlers.

- She calls your love rod "the tinkle gun."

Women

- He answers the phone: "Start talking; it's your dime."

- He likes to brush your teeth.

- He uses your sheets to blow his nose.

- During orgasm he yells out, "Yabba dabba doo!"

- He calls your love nest "the sperm dump."

When Love Turns Bad, Couples Turn Down Memory Lane

Even though their relationship is melting faster than the wicked witch in the Wizard of Oz, couples want to relive those magical moments of puppy love that intoxicated them during the first three hours of their relationship.

Yes, puppy love, when you may not have been in love with the other person, but you sure as hell were in love with *something*. You were so in love, even your shrink got tired of hearing about it. Your pinkies were always linked. In fact, you considered having them soldered together, but you couldn't find a flesh solderer. You had their name tattooed on your arm, right under your ex's — which is now crossed out. You had their nose ring connected to your nose ring — undoing the hook only when one of you caught a cold.

How to Tell if the Love Is Gone

Some Pollyannas don't even realize the relationship is over. If these same people ever jumped off the World Trade Center, at the 50th floor they'd say, "So far, so good."

**You thought my eating habits were cute
when we were first dating.**

That's why it is important to know things are not working out. Fortunately, certain clues tip you off. Your partner starts making weak excuses, like they can't see you because they have to go out and buy milk. **Other clues the love is gone are:**

- He's breathing and that pisses you off.

- You videotape her sleeping to prove her leg crossed over *your* side of the bed.

- She said, "Good morning," but you knew what she meant, so you hit her.

- When you look at him, all you see are his glaring nose hairs.

- A garbage truck careens into a moving van causing a 20-car pile-up, yet the crash fails to drown out her nagging and complaining.

- She steals the batteries out of your remote and puts them in her vibrator.

- You steal her vibrator and replace it with your jumper cables.

- She leaves you for the jumper cables.

Women Turn Love Bad by Complaining

The biggest problem men and women have in understanding each other is that women enjoy a good complaint. On the planet Bras, complaining and communicating are synonymous, and women love to communicate. They believe that complaining burns calories because nice women are usually fatter than the bitchy ones. On Bras the hottest-selling tee shirt says, NO COMPLAIN — NO GAIN. **Things women may complain about are:**

- It's too cold in here.

- It's too hot in here.

- I'm hungry.

- I'm stuffed.

- I have nothing to wear.

- I don't like air.

- It's sunny *again?*

- I don't have anything to complain about.

Women try not to complain for the first couple of dates. This tricks the man into thinking she is different. Unfortunately, all this angst backlogs, and on about the fifth date it comes spewing out faster than a bulimic's Thanksgiving dinner.

....

Women believe that complaining burns calories because nice women are usually fatter than the bitchy ones.

....

Men Turn Love Bad by Being Silent and Resentful

Men think communication is highly overrated. It's like croquet — even if you get good at it, who cares? Men hate to talk because they believe it could lead to marriage. A very common bumper sticker on Penus says, "If God wanted us to talk more, why did he give us genitals?" This is why a man spends most of his time being silent and resentful. His genitals can't talk. Though they do have a primitive form of body language. Up is yes and down is no.

Now that Penusians and Brasserians are living together on Earth, however, men only complain a *little*. Their main complaint is that women complain too much.

What is it about men and their balls?

Miss Communication

Women are obviously better at talking than men. Ever since the cavemen days, men have been the *hunters* while women have been the *hinters*. The earliest word uttered by a woman was a hint, "ahem." The earliest word uttered by a man (which, by the way, did not come for a full century later) was "what?"

Men are coming around, however. They've formed support groups — usually held in pool rooms, but it's a start. And they've begun to read self-help books, like: *I Guess I'm Going to Have to Talk to This Nag Eventually if I Ever Want Sex Again,* and *There Is a Good Chance You Are Talking Because a High-Pitched Shrill Just Drowned Out the Yankee Game.*

. . . .

Ever since the cavemen days, men have been the *hunters* while women have been the *hinters*.

. . . .

By understanding that women are from Bras and men are from Penus, you'll be able to translate what is said into what is actually meant. For example:

When a man says	He means
I wasn't thinking about anything.	I was thinking about sex.
I need my space.	My old girlfriend is in town.
I'll call you in a few days.	My old girlfriend is in town.
I'm going to go out with the guys for a while.	My old girlfriend is in town.

When a woman says	She means
I think we should work on our communication.	There'll be no sex tonight.
Are you listening to me?	If you don't pay attention to me, there'll be no sex tonight.
I don't feel like you love me.	My period is due in one day. Don't even think about sex tonight.
We don't spend enough time together.	I bet it's because that slut, your old girlfriend, is back in town. Don't even think about sex — forever!

The Importance of Humor in Communication

Both women and men claim that a sense of humor is the number one quality they look for in a mate. They want to be sure that when they are dividing their possessions, they can still laugh about it.

Men find nothing funnier than a good fart joke. This amuses even the most educated and sophisticated of men. The Pope would laugh if one of his Bishops ripped one during mass. Women, on the other hand, usually dislike bathroom humor, although they will laugh at certain body functions like: snot, spit, drool, spittle, and phlegm. Generally, liquids that ooze out of the facial area amuse women. For some unknown reason, the word, "boogie" cracks them up.

The following is a man's joke and should *never* be told in the company of a woman — that is if he ever plans on seeing her naked again:

> *What's the definition of eternity? The length of time*
> *between when he comes and she leaves.*

The following is a woman's joke told at a man's expense, and should not be repeated outside the women's arena (which is pretty much anywhere, anytime except a basketball court on Saturday afternoons):

> *Why are men like dogs? They pee standing up, they like to*
> *have their balls licked, and they never vacuum.*

A Quick Communication Quiz for Couples

Most couples need to work on their communication. Take this following quiz to find out just how much work you need to do.

1. **Men:** Your woman said you needed to open up more. Would you say:
   A. "No, leave me alone."
   B. "I'd rather have eye surgery with a pitch fork."
   C. Just nod blankly.

2. **Women:** Your man said you don't respect him. Would you say:
   A. "I respect you just fine. Now, take out the trash."
   B. "There's a booger in your nose."
   C. "Are you breaking up with me?"

3. **Men:** Your woman accused you of not listening to her. Would you say:
   A. "I've been listening to you for five years. You've said nothing."
   B. "Who has that kind of time?"
   C. "What?"

4. **Women:** Your man said "I need my space." Would you say:
   A. "You don't have any."
   B. "So move to Siberia."
   C. "Are you breaking up with me?"

5. **Men:** Your woman said "Tell me your feelings." Would you say:
   A. "I feel like bowling."
   B. "I feel like fishing."
   C. "I feel like having sex — right after I go bowling and fishing."

6. **Women:** Your man said, "Stop nagging me!" Would you say:
   A. "This is talking. You haven't even heard me nag yet, Buster!"
   B. "That's my idea of foreplay."
   C. "Are you breaking up with me?"

Answers: C,C,C,D,C,D & E. Rate yourself:

0 answers right: You can get bacteria in a petri dish at any laboratory.

1 or 2 answers right: You're one Happy Meal away from being a total loser.

3 answers right: Not bad, if you're a guy. If you're a gal, you might be gay.

4 answers right: Good for you. You're so sensitive you'll be heartbroken twice as fast as the average sucker.

How to Turn Love Bad by Becoming a Control Freak

A surefire way to cripple a limping relationship is to try to control it. Control freaks aren't always totalitarian. Sometimes they can be easygoing, saying things like, "Go with the flow…or I'll kill you."

Most Despots are control freaks, such as Kaddafy, Saddam Hussein, or, when you think about it, any ventriloquist. After all, a dummy can't even open its mouth without the ventriloquist's approval. Dummies of the world should unite and write a manifesto called *Dummies for Dummies*.

Control freaks start their own little regime. They only have one person to order around and you're it. They only want kids so they have someone else to bully around. Their first child is always named: MINE.

This "Type A" personality is obsessive and will never let you go. The only way to extricate yourself is to kill them, so good luck. Crime on television is a burgeoning field, so get a movie-of-the-week deal!

How to Criticize Your Partner for Practically Everything

If you are not criticizing every little thing, you should be criticized for missing big opportunities for criticism. The key thing to remember is *there is always something wrong!* So pick on anything and everything.

I'm the man of the house. Don't tell me how to do the dishes!

Appearance. No matter what they're wearing, say, "You're wearing that?" Then do a fake barf followed by wretching sounds. If they are a trendy dresser, say, "You're a spineless fashion-model-wannabe natty twit!" If they *aren't* a trendy dresser, say, "Prisoners of war dress better than you do. Is that part of the Yassar Arafat Spring Collection?"

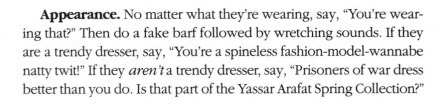

If you are not criticizing every little thing, you should be criticized for missing big opportunities for criticism.

Hygiene. If they are too hygiene conscious, say, "Your place gives me the creeps. It's like the sterile vacuum chamber of a nerve gas research facility." On the other hand, if they are not hygiene conscious, and not brushing, flossing, and gargling three times a day, say, "I'd rather *throw* you a kiss since I don't want to catch the gingivitis-plaque-streptococcus multiplying in your halitosis-filled mouth."

Cooking. Say things like, "What is your forte, burnt spackle?" and "After dinner I'll help you wash the trough." End with, "I'd take a doggie bag, but my dog is picky."

Their home. Their place is either too neat or too sloppy. If the place is too neat, say, "How anal-retentive you are!" Arrive wearing white surgical gloves while sporting those "space outfits" worn by scientists who investigate the ebola virus. If it's sloppy, say, "You're a pig living in a pigsty." Oink every time you stop over. If you have to move your bowels, say, "Could you suggest a room since I can't tell one from another?"

Remember, there is always something wrong!

ARGUING

Arguments are like rivers. If you follow them to the end, you'll find a big mouth. As with everything else, men and women argue with their own unique style.

How Men Argue

Men think arguing is a sport. They do it for fun. Of course they also think it's fun to slam a hockey player into the "boards" causing a concussion. The following is an actual conversation overheard between two men:

— You look like shit. What are you, in love?
— Shut up, you fat fart.
— Hey, lend me five bucks. I'll pay you back next week.
— No way, you still owe me five bucks from last week.
— No I don't; I paid you, you lying scum.
— No you didn't, you asshole. What do you need it for anyway?
— Buy some beer, even though it's your turn, you cheap bastard.
— No it's not, I bought it last week, you lying prick.
— No you didn't. You never buy beer you penny pincher.
— How would you know? You haven't paid attention to anything since the Dodgers took the series.
— Well, shall we go get communion?
— You go first.
— No you.

How Women Argue

Women, on the other hand, do not like to argue with their girlfriends. They will lie, cheat, steal, and blaspheme just to avoid an actual head-on confrontation. For example:

— I heard you told Suzie that I was being a bitch lately.
— No I didn't, she told you that? (SHE DID)
— Yeah.
— She's a liar. (*SHE'S* THE LIAR) You're my best friend. (SUZIE'S HER BEST FRIEND) She's the bitch. (THEY BOTH ARE)

— Yeah, she's the bitch. (THEY ALL ARE)
— Do I look fat in this dress? (SHE DOES)
— No! you look great. (SHE DOES NOT) I love you in Caftans.
— Thanks, and I love you in the mini-skirt and the midriff. The stomach flab is sexy.

They both look fat which is, of course, why they are friends in the *first* place. Suzie, by the way, is losing weight, which is why they are talking about her in the *second* place.

Why Men And Women Argue

There is a very important reason why men and women argue: *if they didn't argue they'd have nothing to say!* It's true. If it weren't for arguments, there'd be silence. Silence scares people. It forces them to reflect and people don't like to reflect. They like to argue.

Of course once an argument begins, it must be resolved or it will resurface like a bad case of herpes. You can't just say, "Oh never mind," and have wild monkey love, hoping he/she will forget about it. The minute the monkey love is over and the bananas are gone, the argument will erupt like a giant cold sore oozing decade-old issues.

The Never Ending Argument

Fortunately, these arguments never end. They are never over. Never ever are they over. They are never never never ever over. That's right — never! For example:

— You don't listen to me.
— I do listen to you.
— No you don't.
— I'm listening to you now.

— Well, of course you're listening to me now 'cause I just said you don't listen to me, so of course you're going to listen to me now.

— Well then, what are you talking about?

— I'm talking about in general you never listen to me.

— Name one time.

— Well, I can't come up with one now, but you never do.

— I hear everything you've ever said.

— Everything?????

— Well, maybe not everything, but mostly everything. Should I start taking notes?

— No, you should start listening to me.

— I do.

— You do?

— I do.

— You do what?

— I do whatever you said I didn't do.

— What'd I say?

— I heard it and I do it.

— You do what, you didn't even hear what I said.

— Never mind.

— Tell me.

— No you tell me.

— No you.

— You.

— You.

— You.

— You.

— You.

— You.

— You.

Drip….Drip…..Drip…Drip…..

Note: This continues until one of them dies of old age. Sometimes the remaining partner will visit the grave site just to continue the argument.

Arguments Are Futile

The reason arguments go on forever is because no one ever wins. Ever. You'll never in a gazillion years hear a man say:

Hmm... you know you're right; I'm wrong. You win the argument. Next time we begin to quarrel, I'm going to listen intently to your side before I fly off the handle like a banshee. I'm so lucky to have such a smart girlfriend. I'm going to go buy you a present.

And you'll never in eternity hear a woman say:

Very good point; I hadn't thought of that. You think of everything. I'm not gonna complain — I mean talk anymore. You talk for me. You do it so much better. Would you like some oral sex now?

This futility is the secret to arguing's charm.

Indications the Two of You Are Mismatched

Arguing is even more futile when the two partners are incompatible. For a relationship to last, the two people must share common interests and common values. **The following couples are doomed from the get-go:**

- She eats chunky. He likes creamy.

- He's a nuclear physicist. She's radioactive.

- He's gay. So's she.

- She's in love with who he can be. He's in love with who she once was.

- He works for Phillip Morris. She has lung cancer.

- She's with the C.I.A. He's with the A.S.P.C.A.

- He's with the I.R.S. She's with the I.R.A.

- She's with the N.R.A. He's an R.N.

- She's a V.I.P. for I.B.M. with an M.B.A. He's an idiot.

- He has a pacemaker. She has an automatic garage-door opener. Every time she comes home, he has a heart attack.

••

In the beginning their looks may have turned your head, but now they turn your stomach.

••

The Party's Over and so Are You

So it's time to face it — you hate your love — a lot! The party's over and all that's left are some warm beers with floating cigarette butts and a bowl of rancid onion dip. And that's how your insides feel. In the beginning their looks may have turned your head, but now they turn your stomach.

Of course, men and women respond to this stage differently. When a man realizes that the love of his life has turned into a swilling vat of toxic mucous, his first response is, "I'm so depressed, she gave great head." When a woman realizes it, her first response is, "I can't believe I'll have to take my clothes off in front of another stranger. I'm so depressed, I think I'll eat a Snickers Bar."

This, of course, is the perfect time to end the relationship. Smart people, when their plane is about to crash, grab a parachute and jump. Dumb people rush off to apply for the job as flight attendant. They figure they can use their partner as a floatation device. If this is your predicament, you are about to enter the next stage: SUFFOCATION. This is when your relationship gets the *clots*.

5

Suffocation
When your relationship clots

Well that's it. You've had it. You're fed up. You're mad as hell and you're not going to fake it anymore. Then you remember how hideous dating is. So you decide to eat on it, eat it over, and eat about it. Instead of finding someone new, you find a new flavor of ice cream to devour: "Rocky Relationship."

You remember that you'd rather be miserable than desperate, and having sex once a month with someone dull is better than getting your tongue caught in a light socket.

Having sex once a month with someone dull is better than getting your tongue caught in a light socket.

Entering the State of Suffocation

The main reason you don't want to start dating again is obvious: it's vomitatious. Dating is like getting an anal probe by an alien.

After they drop you back at your house, you feel so cheap, and nobody will ever believe what just happened to you.

But at least with an alien abduction you have a good story to tell your grandchildren. With dating nobody wants to hear about it. They can top any story you've got.

So, if there is any way to salvage your boring, tedious, lackluster relationship, do so, by all means. Don't pay attention to people telling you there are plenty of fish in the sea. The good fish have all been snatched up and you'll have to wait for them to get thrown back for someone who tastes better. That's why "suffocation" wins hands down over "desperation."

Remember the dictum, "lower your standards!" If they are better than nothing, the relationship is worth saving.

....

**Dating is like getting an anal probe by an alien.
After they drop you back at your house,
you feel so cheap, and nobody will ever believe
what just happened to you.**

....

Reasons Why Men Don't Want to Start Dating Again

When it comes to finding someone new, a smart man realizes that with slim pickings he has a fat chance. **If you're a man, some of the reasons you don't want to start dating again are:**

- You'll have to keep explaining the gashes on your face to other women.

- You'll have to find another woman who puts up with your nocturnal emissions.

- You'll have to find someone else who thinks snoring is a sign of strength.

- You don't know the proper waiting time before you ask for head.

It's hard to believe we've been together for over 32 years.

- You don't want to hold in your farts for the first 10 dates...again!

Reasons Why Women Don't Want to Start Dating Again

Women, too, will reconsider filling out the pink slip when having flashbacks about dating. **If you're a woman you realize:**

- You'll have to work up a smile, and you know that would be a lie.

- If you have to say, "Thank you very much, I had a nice time tonight," you're going to projectile vomit.

- You'll have to do something about the two-inch roots on your head, because a new guy might actually notice.

- You'll have to fake orgasm in front of a complete stranger.

- You've gotten so fat, when you wear your dating spandex, it looks like you're smuggling tuna fish in your ass.

The Peggy Lee Syndrome

So you decide to stay put, even though compared to your current relationship, being hung by your thumbs sounds like a nutty, fun thing to do. Still, you ask the question, "Is that all there is?" reminding you of the song by Peggy Lee. Of course we say, "You should complain, Peggy. At least you had a hit song and you probably got to sleep with some cool musicians. We're dating acne-infested clerks from the 24-hour markets who smell of Slim Jims and Slurpy mix."

Let's face it. You are bored. You are beyond being bored to tears, because you don't even have enough enthusiasm to cry. And you are beyond being bored to death, because at least with death there's an ending — with a nice party and some good potato salad. This boredom goes on forever.

More Chinese water torture. Drip…Drip…Drip…Drip…

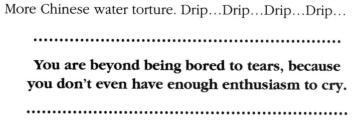

You are beyond being bored to tears, because you don't even have enough enthusiasm to cry.

How to Tell if Your Relationship Is Boring

Have you ever met an old couple that brags their relationship has lasted 65 years? When you ask what they do for excitement, they tell you they sit around the kitchen table and watch each other shrink in size. These people do not realize they are in a boring relationship.

"I just saw my cactus grow," she'll mutter. And she'll spend her whole day eating — gaining so much weight that the only thing she can still get into is her earrings — the clip-ons.

Meanwhile, he's watching the weather channel to see if it's raining in Istanbul. He's so bored he makes a federal case about anything, saying things like, "It's disgusting the way these newsboys hand you the paper. In my day they used to toss it on the porch — treating the rag like the trash it really was!" And he answers the phone on the half-ring, hoping it's the Compost-of-the-Month-Club. "Oh, this month you are offering bat guano and poop from a goose? I'll take two bushels of each."

These people are bored.

Signs Your Relationship Is Boring

- You don't fall asleep after sex, you fall asleep *during* sex.

- You read *TV Guide* with a highlighter and a day planner.

- You find yourself watching a bunionectomy on The Learning Channel.

- There's a sign above your bed that says, "I'd rather be book-keeping."

- You keep saying things like, "Did you say something?"

- Or "Were you going to say something?"

- Or "Could you say something?"

- And then, "Sssshh. I like this commercial."

The good news is that if you are feeling bored, you are feeling *something*. And feeling something is better than feeling nothing at all. So go out and celebrate. Even if you don't feel like it.

If You Are Feeling Bored, Talk about Your Feelings

Love is like a baby's diaper. When it starts to stink, change it. One way to change the relationship is by playing "the feeling game." In the feeling game you talk about your feelings ad nauseam until your conversation becomes more tiresome than a Ken Starr investigation.

All you have to do is begin every sentence with "I feel like." For example:

She: I feel like you don't tell me your feelings.

He: I feel like lying on the couch.

She: I feel like that's not really a feeling.

He: It sure feels like one.

She: I feel like you don't love me anymore.

He: I feel like you hid the remote.

She: I feel like you're not listening to me.

He: I feel like a cold beer.

She: I feel like you're confusing "wants" with "feelings."

He: Who died and made you the Feeling Czar?

She: I feel like that wasn't a feeling.

He: I feel like carving your face like a pumpkin and shoving a candle up your ass.

She: I feel like you're not getting this.

Notice how effectively this exercise kills time and, at the same time, adds warmth and sharing to an otherwise comatose relationship.

How to Turn a Boring Same-Old-Shit Relationship into a Depressing, Therapy-Provoking Fate Worse than Death

Just because your relationship is in a coma, doesn't mean you have to pull the plug. There are many things you can do to stir things up again. Look at it this way: you're like an old pot of chili. Your bottom's crusty and your beans are burnt. But stir up that pot of chili and what have you got? Stirred up crusty burnt shit!

So get out there and make things happen. Go into group therapy. Find people sicker than you. Go into marriage counseling, but when they offer advice, put your hands over your ears and sing, "la la..la...la..." Go to twelve-step meetings like Bored-to-Death Anonymous, then come home and break people's anonymity just for laughs. By the way, laughter is supposed to boost your immune system and help fight cancer. They're having a hard time proving this theory, because it turns out laboratory mice have lousy senses of humor.

How to Make a Doomed Relationship Fun and Interesting

You were on the Love Boat, but then it hit an iceberg, causing it to sink to the bottom. And you have no life boat. Or a pot to piss in. Is that a cause for concern? Yes, but who cares? The musicians played as the Titanic sank and so can you. **There are many ways of making a doomed relationship fun and interesting. For example:**

- Get married. You'll argue about the wedding plans and arguing is fun.

- Have a child. As soon as it is old enough, train it to entertain you like an organ grinder monkey.

- Have a child and tell them they are adopted.

- Adopt a child and tell them you are their real parent.

...And so the human says, "I thought you said a 12-inch pianist." Get it? A 12-inch pianist. Hey, are you an audience or an oil painting? Is this mike on?

- Write an adoption screenplay and have it adapted for television.

- Adopt seven children and name them do, re, me, fa, so, la, ti.

- Train the children to perform *The Sound of Music* and then take the show on the road. If the children get the flu, change the title to *The Sound of Mucous*.

Why *Being* Committed Is Worse Than *Getting* Committed

At this point in the relationship you've decided to tie the knot, not realizing the knot is a noose around your neck. That's what couples do when they're in a drab relationship for too long. Rather than end it, they pump up the commitment level. Then they have a gaggle of kids, hoping to lose each other in the crowd. This is insane. People try to correct their mistakes by upping the stakes, which is the biggest mistake they can make. It's like putting out a fire with hair spray. You end up with a raging forest fire. And flat hair.

People try to correct their mistakes by upping the stakes, which is the biggest mistake they can make.

RULES FOR LIVING TOGETHER

When living together, rule number one is: "The woman is the man of the house." You don't believe it? Then why do all the men in the world put the seat down after they pee? Because women tell them to. Why isn't it the woman's job to leave the seat *up* after they're done? Simple. Because the roost is ruled by a hen, not a cock. Yes, even the cock is ruled by a hen.

This is why men escape the roost — to avoid becoming "hen-whipped" and "pussy-pecked" — heading outside to find any activity that doesn't involve a woman — unless she's taking her clothes off on a stage.

Rules for Living Together for Men

1. **Don't leave your curly little chest and pubic hairs all over the sink and bathtub.** If you have to shower, wear a wet suit to contain these little hairs. There should be a law against these hairs, and when women make up the majority in Congress, there will be!

2. **Don't give your new number out to old girlfriends.** If they call, there *will* be trouble.

3. **Don't take the side of the bed closest to the bathroom.** She will be climbing over you to pee for the rest of your life. Women's bladders are smaller, they pee more. Urine a relationship, start peeing attention to these things.

4. **During her menstrual cycle, do not say, "Ew."**

Counting my condoms again, Harriet?
Do you even remember what they look like?

5. **If there is a noise in the middle of the night, don't say, "You go, you're the boss."** Even if you're a prick, if she went and got whacked by an axe murderer, you would really feel bad for many years.

6. **Condense your personal belongings to one sock drawer and three hangers, because that is all you will get.**

7. **Do not bring anything to the home that you do not want her to see.** Anything in her house is her business. In fact, most women invite men to move in with them just so they can go through their things. The first night you go out with the boys, know that she is rummaging through your sock drawer. This is gospel. This is why men eventually begin to stay home more — to stand guard over their sock drawer.

Rules for Living Together for Women

The rules for women are whatever they make them up to be. She's the boss. She makes them up as she goes along. Even if this causes the man to leave, in her next relationship she'll still be the boss.

CONSIDERING THE POSSIBILITY OF MARRIAGE

Marriage can be boring, but that's no reason not to take the leap. Go ahead. Get married. Move to the suburbs. Buy a station wagon. Have 2.5 kids. Name them Jason, Elizabeth and Bar – – –.
Just make sure you marry for the right reason: the tax break.

Not Good Enough Reasons for Women to Get Married

- You're thinner than you've ever been.
- You finally found a best friend who can wear mauve.
- You like to "hokey pokey" with old people.
- You need a new blender.

- Your grandmother is going to die soon.

- Your last name is O'Schmickelstein and his is better — O'Schmickelfarkle.

- You've got health insurance and he needs his spleen cleaned.

Not Good Enough Reasons for Men to Get Married

- You have no plans for Saturday Night.

- You've got a coupon for 10% off on a tux.

- There was a freeze in the Midwest and orchids are cheap.

- You have the hots for the maid of honor.

- Your cousin's three-piece accordion band really needs a gig.

- Her travel visa's up and there's a firing squad waiting for her in Equador.

How to Propose

Once you decide to get married, there is nothing more important to a woman's long-term disillusionment than a memorable proposal. That is why a man's proposal must be storybook, picture perfect. After all, you are asking a woman if you can take over the job of making her life miserable from now on, so take a minute and plan the thing. Be romantic.

The Setting: Where you propose is just as important as what you're proposing. Never propose in the laundromat, for example. With all the noise from the washers and dryers, the words, "Will you marry me" will sound like "Can I borrow some soap?" Therefore, choose a quiet, romantic setting that reflects what it will be like married for the rest of your lives. We suggest a cemetery.

The Timing: Timing is everything. In the cemetery try to propose in the daytime, not during a full moon, because if creatures start rising from their graves, she might say, "No."

The Posture: It is always good to get down on one knee when proposing. So don't propose in church, she'll think you are praying — which might be true. You might be praying that she turns you down. Also don't propose in the bedroom. When you get down on one knee, she'll think you're trying to perform oral sex — which also might be true, but that could wait for a couple of minutes. And kneel by a stone with a beautiful inscription. Don't pick one that says, I NEVER THOUGHT THE BITCH WOULD KICK THE BUCKET. I HOPE SHE ROTS IN HELL.

The Words: Always say, "Will you marry me <u>Hildegarde</u>." Make sure you remember her name. And don't try to be flamboyant. You're not Cyrano De Bergerac making up love poems. If you improvise, you'll probably sound like a dork. For example:

Hey, you know, like, well, I've been thinking and stuff and, well, like, you know, we've been going together for a while and everything, and well, so, I was wondering if, you know, like maybe the two of us should, you know, maybe try out what it might be like if the two of us were, you know, married and stuff, and well, like I was wondering, you know, like what you thought of the idea and stuff, whether you'd, you know, also like to be married and everything as well, you know, like, so, I don't know, what do you think?

Give it a rest, Shakespeare. Thou sucketh the big one! Just go by the book and you can improvise when you become poet laureate for the 7th bag boys reunion of your local supermarket.

The Prenuptial Agreement

Once you decide to get married, prenuptial agreements are a necessity. There's a 65 percent chance your marriage will end up in the toilet. So be prepared. Rich people invented the prenuptial agreement and rich people are generally smart — that's why they're rich.

It's the dumb ones that have no money, going around saying, "Money isn't everything" or "At least I have my health." Idiots who think they have their health generally have a heart attack trying to pay their bills. They never have enough insurance to cover the attack because they thought they had their health. Well, guess what? Sick rich people can afford to buy poor people's organs and get healthy. They don't need their health.

Even if you're living in a trailer park outside of a slice-and-dice-o-matic plant in Indiana and all you own is a pot holder stained with Chef Boyardee sauce from last night's spaghetti dinner, and a ten-inch black-and-white TV with a coat-hanger antenna, you still need a prenuptial agreement. Because no matter how little you have, you'll still fight over it when you break up.

It's never about money or possessions, it's always about spite, and spite knows no boundaries. One of you gets the TV and the other gets the pot holder. It's that simple. In fact, that's how you'll know if you're being left. If you wake up and the TV's gone, so is Charlie. He took it — just for spite.

And it's not polite to ask for your gifts back. Anything you gave should be theirs. Don't say, "Hey I gave you that velvet painting of the dogs playing poker. It's mine." Don't be an Indian giver. You gave it to her. You bought it at Fred Tucker's garage sale for $2. You wrapped it up in old fish paper and you presented it to her because you loved her. Let her have it. It still smells like carp anyway.

You know that golf ball cleaner that you gave him for Valentine's Day and he immediately tried it out on his testicles? Don't be rude and ask for it back — it's his. Fair is fair. Besides, it still smells like carp anyway.

At this point if you are not making plans to marry, or not moving in together, or don't even know your partner's second name, or you have moved in together and you miss your friends, or you did get married and the last good time you had was at the wedding, you may be ready to consider leaving the relationship. You have finally come to the conclusion that nothing is better than them. You're about to enter the next stage of dating: EVACUATION. This is when you get the *trots*.

6

Evacuation
When you get the trots

At this point in the relationship, you realize something's rotten in the state of Denmark. And you can smell it in Des Moines. It could be hormones, it could be a mid-life crisis, or it could be that every time you look at your partner, you throw up. Whatever it is, the idea of being single again is as appealing as a prison break to an inmate on death row. The process often begins with jealousy.

The idea of being single again is as appealing as a prison break to an inmate on death row.

How to Use Jealousy to Start Ending the Relationship

Jealousy is the perfect fight starter. It can set two people off faster than a Zippo lighter in the Hindenberg. It speeds the sinking ship to the bottom. It's like after the Titanic hits the iceberg, you smack it with a torpedo.

For example, he's jealous of her dog because she tongue-kisses it and he had to take her out five time before he could do the same — in spite of the differences in breeding: his ancestors came over on the Mayflower, while the dog is a mutt.

She's jealous of only one thing, though that one thing could be a waitress, a secretary, a bag lady, or the Super Bowl. Women don't trust men. A husband could be in a coma hooked up to life support, and she would still suspect the nurse because she inserted his catheter.

Jealousy is particularly choice for sick obsessive-compulsive people who fight like hell just so they can have wild lustful "I'm so sorry sex" afterwards. This is like banging your head against the wall because it feels good when you stop — after which you can be banged against the wall by your partner — providing you don't complain of a headache.

....

Jealousy can set two people off faster than a Zippo lighter in the Hindenberg...It's like after the Titanic hits the iceberg, you smack it with a torpedo.

....

How to Tell if Your Partner Is Cheating on You

Most people swear they would know if their little "snookems" was cheating on them. Bob swears there is no way Kathy would have an affair, while Kathy scoffs at the idea that Bob would ever sleep with someone else. Meanwhile Bob and Kathy are both playing "hide the salami" on the side.

When Bob finds out Kathy's been unfaithful, he is outraged and unable to concentrate on the football game — for the first quarter. When Kathy finds out, she's so mad she runs away — for five minutes. Then she returns because Bob is hungry. Neither mentions it because they don't speak to each other. After all, speaking could lead to communication.

Sorry I'm late, honey, but I was shopping and I just lost track of time.

Fortunately, you don't have to wait as long as Bob or Kathy. **Hints the person you are seeing is cheating on you are:**

- He comes back from the office wearing a different suit than when he left.

- He comes back from the office wearing a bathrobe.

- He doesn't come back from the office at all.

- Your parrot keeps repeating, "I told you not to call me here. I told you not to call me here."

- She stays out all night raising money for the Save the Rat Foundation.

- She goes out for a quart of milk and when she comes back, there's a new President.

- There are more people in the bed when you get up than when you went to sleep.

How to Encourage Your Partner to Cheat on You

The oldest trick in the book is to make your partner dump you so you don't have to dump them, so ask yourself whether you'd rather be the dumper or the dumpee. Ask not what you can do for your dumper, but what your dumper can do for you. And after you're done conjugating, what your dumper can do for you is to make you look good by being the dumpee. And then let the games begin. Post a sign saying, DUMPING ALLOWED. **Help them have affairs — then catch them in the act. Try these sure-fire ways:**

- Give him subtle, subliminal hints like, "Our waitress is cute. You could nail her on the first date."

- Distribute naked wallet-sized pictures of her to the Navy.

- Post her name on the Internet if anyone searches under the key word, "promiscuous."

- Post his name on the Internet if anyone searches under the key words, "hung like a horse."

How to Catch Your Partner at Cheating

Now that you've encouraged your partner to cheat on you, it's important to catch them in the act. You can't become the dumpee unless you prove they're the dumper. Catching your partner is easier than you think. If you watch Columbo and Dick Tracy (private eyes), or Ken Starr (private thighs), you're ready to start your own sleezy PI firm. **These are the simple skills you'll need to make yourself the chump of the dump:**

- Make an at-home DNA kit with a popsickle stick and a cotton ball.

- Collect sperm samples with a turkey baster without your partner knowing.

- Bug their office with video cameras.

- Bug their car with microphones.

- Bug their home with roaches and termites.

- Trace phone calls.

- Trace steps.

- Trace their body's outline with chalk.

Remember, they've been bugging you for years, it's time to bug them!

How to Use Insults to Start Relationship-Breaking Arguments

Now that you've dowsed your partner with lighter fluid, all you need is a match. That's why insults are so important. Insults can ignite the dead wood of your relationship, giving your latest flame third-degree burns. While criticism may injure your partner, these lines will help you add insult to injury.

Busting the Balls of the Bastard

Insulting a man is easy for a woman. She learned from a pro — her mother. Nagging, nit-picking, and name-calling come naturally for a woman. Women don't even need a sparring partner. A woman can pick a fight with a man who's not even on the same continent. Let's face it, a woman could pick a fight with mold!

Women know that a man's Achilles' Heel is his **sexual prowess,** so whenever possible, **she should hit below the belt with the following lines:**

- The next time you're making love to me, let me know.

- I've gotten better foreplay at a pap smear.

- You're a lousy lay — just like your father.

- I'm not saying you don't move well in bed, but you could get into medical school as a cadaver.

- Out of ten million sperm, I can't believe *you* won.

- There used to be something I liked about you, but I spent it.

- Why don't you shove the remote up your ass — then you can change channels while you fart.

••

**Insulting a man is easy for a woman.
She learned from a pro — her mother.**

••

How to Put the Bitch in Her Place

In fighting women are far more powerful and clever than men. That's why a man needs to aim for her Achilles' Heel, her **appear-**

You want a divorce? OK. Which half of the fish would you like?

ance. He should keep flinging fat comments her way. Eventually, this makes every woman cry. Margaret Thatcher was once overheard asking the House of Commons if her thighs were too big. Even a super model like Kate Moss thinks she's pudgy.

Here is some fire for your fuel:

- That's not a backside, that's a backyard.

- No, you're not fat. Just be sure to fluff up the metal chair when you stand up.

- Good news! The government just declared your body a Federal Disaster Area.

- With your looks you could get a job modeling for death threats.

- I hear the Post Office gave your ass its own zip code.

- The Federal Phlegm Foundation called. You're their new poster girl.

- The next time you take a drink of water, could you leave the toilet seat down?

They Say that Breaking Up Is Hard to Do

The final stage of a relationship, the evacuation, is the hardest and the most inevitable. Finally, you remember why you've been single for the better part of the millennium — *love stinks!* Love is like a stopped-up toilet, and it's time for your plumber to call for back up. It's at least time to have that tattoo of their face removed from your butt. Yes, it's time to put *them* out of *your* misery.

But it must be done with finesse because "breakin' up is hard to do" and, contrary to Paul Simon, "just slippin' out the back, Jack" ain't an option. Even though you want to hop on the bus, Gus, and don't mean to be coy, Roy, *just stop the damn singing and get a plan, Fran!*

....

**Love is like a stopped-up toilet and it's time
for your plumber to call for back up.**

....

Reasons Why You Really Should Break Up

Let's face it. You're past the forgiving phase of the relationship —
still mad about the time she slammed you with her car, and then
sued you for breaking her windshield. And she's still mad at you
for sleeping with her best friends. She really misses them.

**So it's time to hit the road, Jack. And here are just a few
reasons why:**

- He's seeing someone else.

- He got the baby-sitter pregnant — and you don't even have
  kids.

- She makes you sick.

- You fantasize about hitting her in the face with an ice pick.

- You haven't had sex since the fall of Saigon.

- He overflowed the bathtub — with other women.

Revenge Is Good

The minute women realize a relationship is kaput, they call for
support. They call in the" Uh-Oh" squad. At the Uh-Oh Summit,
the unanimous decision is — cry! Then they all sob together, blub-
bering all over each other. Women cry; they like it. Women also
like to take long suffering rehabs, milking it for every pint of pity
they can get. Women take themselves out to romantic dinners,
order a bottle of wine, and sit in the corner of the café and weep.
Women weep. Men sleep. Women like to weep to sad songs on
the radio (sad songs say so much). They play Michael Bolton 'til

their tear ducts dry up and then eventually rebel and start spitting out venomous foam instead of tears. This foam denotes that phase two of the breakup is about to begin — revenge!

Revenge is good for a woman. It's biblical, for God sakes. Revenge is the only true way to recover from the heartbreak of heartbreak.

....

Revenge is the only true way to recover from the heartbreak of heartbreak.

....

Ways Women Can Get Revenge

- Burn his CD collection, saying, "I thought you had already listened to them."

- Throw out the autographed Babe Ruth ball caught at Yankee Stadium by his grandfather.

- Sleep with his business partners.

- Tell his mother *everything* he said about her.

- Finally lose the weight he's begged you to for five years.

- Pose nude for *Playboy*.

- Invest the *Playboy* money in Viagra stock and make millions.

- Write a tell-all book, telling all he had an enlargement and doubled his penis size — to two inches.

Ways Men Can Get Revenge

Actually, men don't generally get into revenge. They usually get into another woman — pretty quickly. In fact, they usually overlap their women like shingles on a roof. Of course, that's *their* revenge; they've already replaced you.

Congratulations!

Well, congratulations. You made it. You did it. You got rid of them. You've unshackled yourself from the chains and slavery of your relationship. Good job! Reward yourself with a pat on the head and a small piece of cheese. Take a moment to pray for those poor suffering dolts who are still in love.

This is your commencement. Instead of Pomp and Circumstances sing Pimp and Circumsize. Go ahead, be bitter — it's chic. Bitter is better. Whatever you do, don't worry about being alone on New Year's Eve, and don't even think about the possibility of sleeping alone for the rest of your miserable life — that's tomorrow's thoughts. After all, tomorrow is another problem.

Yes, you are ready to move on with your life — to make a new start. You've graduated from that starter relationship, ready to embark on the mature relationship — the real one. That other one was just practice. That's right. We can help you. We can help you find someone lonely to make miserable.

So turn the page, go ahead. Guess what? Life is a game of Monopoly and you're back to "GO." So reread chapter one. You are now ready for the next stage of dating: DESPERATION! This is when your love life *rots*.

DEBBIE KASPER

Debbie Kasper is a stand-up comic and writer. She is a two-time Emmy nominee for her writing on *The Rosie O'Donnell Show.* Before that she was a writer for the sitcom, *Roseanne.* She received the prestigious Drama-Logue award for her one-woman show, *Without Me, My Show is Nothing.* On television, she has appeared on *VH-1's Stand-up Spotlight, Lifetime's Girls' Night Out,* and *A&E's Evening at the Improv.* She currently resides in Santa Monica, California.

ELLIOT SULLIVAN

Elliot Sullivan is a stand-up comic, writer, therapist, and publisher. He co-authored the critically-acclaimed *Women are from Bras, Men are from Penus.* He has appeared on *Showtime's Comedy Club Network* and *The Everyday Show with Joan Lunden.* Holding two degrees from Cornell University, he is a licensed trainer and co-developer of NLP. He currently resides in New York City.

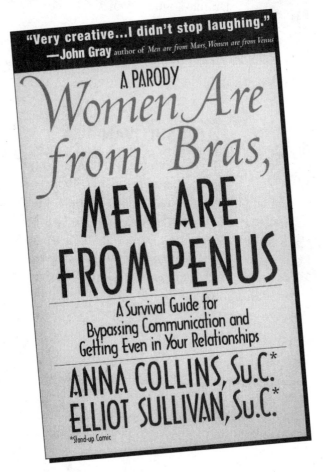